Going About Cruising

Going About Cruising

Andrew Simpson

WATERLINE

Published by Waterline Books
an imprint of Airlife Publishing Ltd
101 Longden Rd, Shrewsbury, England

ISBN 1 85310 293 8

A Sheerstrake production.

A CIP catalogue record of this book
is available from the British Library

CONTENTS

ACKNOWLEDGEMENTS

In my researches for this book, I have found many people generous with their expertise and time. Of these I would particularly like to thank Robert Curry of the American Bureau of Shipping; Robin Duchesne, Edmund Whelan, Robin Sjoberg and Belinda Stannage of the RYA; and Stephen Alcock, Ken Webb, and Jools Bennett of the Island Cruising Club. I would also like to thank George Hayes for entrusting his yacht Fairlight to me, and Anne Walton for reading the first draft and for her heroic struggles with a camera. Finally, my special gratitude must go to my wife Chele, who made it all possible, and my daughter Claire who made it all necessary.

THE AUTHOR

Born in India in 1940, Andrew Simpson has been continuously involved with the sea and sailing since he joined a training ship at the age of thirteen. After service in the Merchant Navy, he designed his first boat in 1967 and, in 1970, completed the Round Britain Race in his 26' trimaran Three Fingered Jack. Since then, over twenty different designs, have taken to the water.

Sailing has taken him over 30,000 miles, around European and Mediterranean waters, across the Atlantic, through the Caribbean and Bahamian islands, and in the United States where he lived for five years.

Now, when not pursuing his profession as a yacht surveyor in Poole, Andrew continues to design the type of boats which interest him. In addition to this technical work, he also writes radio plays for the BBC and, in company with his wife Chele, continues to cruise his 31' sloop Spook as often as they can escape.

Chapter 1
THE DREAM

For those of us with a recurring urge to escape the general clamour, there aren't a lot of convenient places left. True, the Himalayas or the Sahara still offer the kind of contemplative solitude many of us crave, but they are certainly not accessible on a casual basis, say for a long weekend or the span of fortnight's holiday.

It is inevitable in our modern world that, the greater and more mobile our population, the more the fragile ecology must be protected from our ravages. It is for the good of our planet that we are penned into urban enclosures and discouraged from straying over what little is left of our wildernesses. And, when we venture out, we must tramp in the footsteps of others, guided along carefully delineated paths, seeing but seldom touching. It is as if a gigantic 'Keep Off The Grass' sign were suspended over our land — and laudable that this be so.

So, where can we go — those who do not care for footprints? How can we travel where the wounds of our passing heal behind us? The answer, of course, is simple. Thousands follow the impulse. We go to sea.

I remember as a child, shortly after the war, standing on the beach at Folkestone and thinking that the water that lapped the shingles ran unbroken to the place of my birth, Bombay. Even then it struck me that here was the universal path, the road to wherever I wished to be. I could touch it with my hand and feel the distant resonances of every continent, hear faint echoes of the various tongues, taste the dust and smell the heavy air. At the age of seven, the ability to drive a car seemed a feat of magic, quite beyond even my most fanciful imaginings. But I *could* sail — I knew I could! The process was obvious and the skills, I thought, easily acquired. All I needed was a boat and a little understanding from my family. Then I could journey wherever my fancy led me!

And I still regard sailing as the most natural way to travel.

Perhaps at this stage it would be useful to try to define what cruising under sail actually means — or, more precisely, what it means to me, for we all have our own views on the matter. To think of it simply as visiting places in a sailing boat will not do. In the 1970 Round Britain Race I visited (and had a memorably riotous time in) Plymouth, Crosshaven in Ireland, Barra in the Outer Hebrides, Lerwick in the Shetland Isles, and Lowestoft in Norfolk. Despite the fact that there was both satisfaction and, to a lesser extent, enjoyment in circumnavigating the British Isles, in no way could the whole grisly experience be thought of as 'cruising'. Although having initially been conceived to promote short-handed cruising design, the Round Britain Race remained very much a 'race' with all that meant in terms of competitive pressure.

The next year was to prove no more comfortable for me. Having sold my boat, I was eager for a temporary berth and had the misfortune to sign on with a man whose aim it was to see how far along the coast we could day-sail in a week. We embarked in Salcombe and headed east. My 'Skipper' (for thus he liked to be addressed) was, by his own estimation, a wizard at working the tides. And his determination never to miss a fair one brought a potentially happy crew to the brink of mutiny.

The weather was relentlessly foul. But our man never wavered. Onwards we slogged, plunging from port to port. Our skipper scorned all discomfort and made light of the punishment we were dealing the boat. I can see him now, hunched over the chart table, his oilskins slick with water, pricking off our progress with manic glee.

The crunch finally came in Dover. After another awful day at sea followed by a disappointing meal ashore, we were awoken before daybreak with the rousing news that if we sailed immediately and rode the flood tide we would be in Ramsgate by breakfast. As we had all trudged back from that unspeakable Tandoori house hardly more than four hours previously, and our stomachs still churned with the results of that expedition, the news wasn't well received. The rain still pelted down, the wind still howled. Even the fishermen were staying at home, witnessed by the fleet of battered trawlers moored safely against the quay. When these blatant signals of nature's discouragement were brought to the attention of our skipper, he was at first astonished at our wimpishness, and then indignant at our refusal to turn to.

This, I felt, was not a man who understood what cruising was all about. There was confusion in his mind between what was possible to achieve and what was important to enjoy. It isn't beholden upon yachtsmen to behave like whipping friars, bent on mortification of the flesh for the good of their souls. Their sport is quite tough enough without making it mindlessly intolerable.

Closer to my ideal, but still not entirely according with what I believe to be the true essence of cruising, was the voyage Jenny (my first wife) and I made from England to Texas in 1974. We were then refugees from the crippling strike-afflicted economy of that era, and were impatient to reinstate our boatbuilding business in a new land. Again there was no lack of diversion on the way. Madeira, St. Kitts, Grand Cayman, and finally Galveston, all obligingly trotted out their various allurements and we tasted of them as time permitted. But, *again*, our itinerary was controlled by outside influences; there were potential customers to visit *en route*, the children joining us in Houston on a prescribed date, and, most urgently, the need to breath life into our dwindling earnings without delay. In a way we were still racing — not against other boats or a pointless goal this time, but against a schedule every bit as constraining.

By contrast, in 1978 I was to return to the West Indies in more relaxed circumstances. With a divorce and a flurry of other minor catastrophes behind me, I was again without a boat and sorely in need of the therapeutic balm of a few weeks at sea. Fortunately, I had recently met Chele who, along with her other conspicuous charms, was then the owner of a fibreglass 40 footer (12.19m) named *Vaquero*.

Accompanied by our great friends, Bruce and Martha Wild, we set sail from Galveston to cross the Gulf of Mexico. In the lightest of breezes, we virtually drifted across, taking eleven days to cover the nine-hundred-odd miles. The heat was merciless. By the time we eventually arrived in Key West we were, in the vernacular of the sea, good and ready to 'make and mend'. We played tennis, quaffed ice-cold beer at Sloppy Joe's Bar (of Hemingway fame), and toured the surrounding region on rented bicycles. After a few days of this welcome recreation, restlessness set in and we continued on our way, carrying the eastbound Gulf Stream around the tip of Florida to Bimini in the Bahamas.

Sailing amongst those magical islands can only be described as sublime. The water is as clear as glass and graded in colour from brilliant aquamarine to the most delicate turquoise in the shallows. The route from Bimini to New Providence takes you over the Great Bahama Bank where the depth is never more than a few feet. Rolling along at seven knots, with the coral heads flashing by only inches from your keel, takes a bit of getting used to, but it is a glorious sensation, nonetheless.

To say that we were enjoying ourselves would be a paltry understatement. The scenery was dazzling and the company always congenial. We swam naked amongst the coral and potted with .22 rifles at balloons cast astern in our wake. Off Nassau we were obliged to dodge a waterspout. Later, in the Exhumas, we lurked in Highborne Cay whilst hurricane *Juliet*, out in the Atlantic, made her mind up as to which way she was heading. In Clarence Town, Long Island, we participated rather too enthusiastically in the Columbus Day goombay (party) and had to lay up for a while to recuperate. For all of us it was a period of enchantment and personal growth. We found peace and excitement and great stimulation, all in generous measure. From the cruising standpoint, this was definitely it.

Vaquero becalmed on the Great Bahama Bank. Note the home made vane gear which steered faultlessly for over 2000 miles.

And so was an Easter week I once spent pottering around the Solent in a minute plywood bilge-keeler. From Beaulieu to Bursledon, we sailed by day and crept into muddy creeks by night. Almost penniless, we cooked over a temperamental paraffin stove, saving what meagre resources we had for spending in the local pubs (illicitly, I seem to recall, for we must have been under age). Those were days of high adventure, all contained within a few miles radius.

For cruising has nothing to do with scale — it doesn't become more so simply by widening its range. The lad in his tiny boat is as genuinely bent on cruising as any hardened voyager. Although blue water sailing may be the ultimate goal, there is no reason why less ambitious trips should not yield as much pleasure in the meantime. It's important that cruising should not be thought of as exclusively a long distance exploit. The bays and inlets of our own shores are rich with interest. A person could spend a lifetime exploring them. But, should that not be enough, or when time and funds permit, the coastline of continental Europe lies only a few hours sailing away, as different and as exotic in its own right as any Pacific isle.

It has become my opinion that cruising has more to do with exploration than it has to do simply with journeying. The benefits are gained as much in what lies ashore as in the sailing itself — perhaps more so. Maybe it is the motive rather than the means which distinguishes it from other kinds of sailing. For those who are interested, it provides the opportunity to view the world through a lens of startling clarity. And for those who are inquisitive, it provides an unparalleled chance to meet other people on a more or less random basis and, often, to see them at their best.

Let me give you an example.

Mallorca — an island of stunning beauty and great cynicism, where charm and avarice live side by side. To arrive at Palma airport is to be sucked into an exquisitely refined process which will deftly part you from your money. Taxi drivers, shopkeepers, hoteliers and restauranteurs, will all dip their hands so painlessly into your pocket you will think you've had an anaesthetic. To most of them you are simply another tourist — a crop to be harvested. The Mallorcans are not naturally heartless but, like most of us, they have become adept at earning their livelihood without too many awkward pangs of conscience.

But, whilst the tourist will always be fair game, the cruising sailor — so long as he remains courteous and abides by the rules — seems to arrive with different credentials, as though through a door marked 'friend'.

Of course, it is inevitable in a place like Mallorca that tourism will have pervaded every coastal town to some extent, but none have become as grim as the conurbation that fringes Palma Bay. Thankfully, away from the ghastly concrete cliffs of the high-rise hotels and apartments, there are places of wonderful tranquillity. Strung around the coast are dozens of sheltered *calas* and sweeping sandy bays where one can anchor, often in total solitude, out of sight and sound of neon signs and blaring discotheques.

A favourite port of call for Chele and me is Porto Petro, situated on the south-east coast. It is a tiny town with a reasonable anchorage, almost totally invisible from seaward. Typically, the traditional activities of fishing and agriculture, although still extant, have been nudged aside to make way for the more immediate rewards of the tourist trade. The waterfront is a line of small gift shops, restaurants and bars — all fairly inoffensive in their lack of stridency. One such place goes under the name of *Pepe's Cafe*, a cheap and cheerful establishment leaning heavily towards the chips-with-everything end of the market.

Since returning to Europe, Chele and I have cruised the Balearics a number of times, and usually make a point of spending at least a couple of days in Porto Petro to take advantage of the convenient supply of fresh (though unfortunately non-potable) water on the quay, and the well-stocked *supermercado* not far distant. On these occasions we always patronise *Pepe's Cafe*. The breakfasts are substantial and the coffee superb.

Coming in to anchor in Mallorca. Not a tourist in sight.

And, notably, despite the hordes of tourists who must tramp through during the course of a season, and the infrequency of our visits, for some reason we *never* go unrecognised. Paco, or one of his fellow waiters, will come bounding out of the shadows to pump our hands, enquire about our health, the state of the boat, and — as an afterthought — to take our order.

On our last visit we had rowed ashore to find the local bank closed for the *siesta*. Short of cash, cheated of the cold beers we had set our hearts on, we hung gloomily around in the fierce afternoon sun deciding what to do. Paco's shout from across the street drew our attention.

Our Spanish is far from fluent but, with much gesticulation and apologetic shrugs, we did what we could. *'No tenemos dinero. El banco esta cerrado.'* We went on to explain that we were planning to sail before nightfall, and would have to wait until the next port before we would be in funds again.

Paco scorned our reluctance to join him at the cafe. Taking Chele by the arm, he led us to a vacant table. *'No pay problema! Me pagas el ano que viene!'* — pay me next year.

Or the year after that would have done, I dare say. To my mind it would have been inconceivable that he would have trusted us so fully, had we arrived by bus or taxi. And Paco is by no means alone. Over the years, in many parts of the world, from people speaking many different tongues, we have received more kindness than we could possibly record here. Why this should be so, I don't really understand, but my guess is that it touches on that instinct to wander which is latent in all of us. It could be that the cruising sailor, as he comes ashore with his scorched face and faded clothes, triggers the imagination in those more tethered by their responsibilities. He is, perhaps, the vicarious champion of their dreams, perceived as being successful in that great quest for the freedom many of us desire.

In the following pages I hope to assist, advise, and inspire you. Because it's the only possible way to handle such a subject, this is a thoroughly self-opinionated book. What follows is what we have learned. Others have learned otherwise and their views will probably differ. At the end of the day it will be up to you to weigh up the alternatives and to follow your instincts.

After all, that is what it's all about, isn't it?

Chapter 2

THE CHOICE

Wherever two or more yachtsmen are gathered together, there you have the makings of an argument about boat types. It is an issue as personal and as potentially contentious as the choice of a spouse. Every person has his opinions, his preferences, and his prejudices. And every person is usually eager to voice them.

Listen in at any yacht club and the conversational alignments will emerge. The wooden boat man likes to consider himself an aristocrat, entitled to sniff at other baser forms of construction. The fibreglass sailor tends to command the maritime middle class, content for his boat to be a clone of many others. Our man of steel sees himself as the hard case of the tribe, his own character as dauntless as his craft. The ferro-cement boat owner, so they say, plays the peasant, his lumbering vessel purchased for no other reason than economy. And, even beyond that awful pail, is the multihull sailor, clinging to the lunatic fringe, hurtling around at speeds considered disgraceful by his soberer fellows.

These are stereotypes, of course, and embedded in them is both truth and fallacy.

But it should be self-evident that, no matter how apparently outlandish they may seem to others, any type of boat or method of construction that has endured long enough to collect its share of devotees must obviously have some redeeming virtues. If a boat has nothing to offer, then it rapidly joins the dodo in extinction.

The aim of this chapter is to underline how vital it is for the would-be cruising sailor to make the right choices. The type of boat he chooses, its cost, its rig, and the material used in its construction, can all have profound effects upon its suitability. A boat which may be perfect for one style of sailing could be hopeless in another. To cross the Great Bahama Bank in a vessel drawing ten feet (3.05m) would be the stuff of nightmares. To take a large trimaran, whose beam almost equals its length, into a Cowes marina in high summer would be to see the blood drain from the berthing master's face.

The old design adage that 'form follows function' should be a useful principle for yachtsmen contemplating their options. It couldn't be simpler, one would think. Define the type of sailing you are going to do, add some financial parameters and a pinch or two of aesthetic preference, and the choice of boat will pop up naturally.

Sheevra and Giralda, two beautifully maintained classic yachts.

In theory such a scheme should work nicely. In reality it often founders on the problem some people experience in identifying their requirements. For the yachting business is dream business and, all too often, the emotive power of this dream can obliterate more rational mental processes.

Take the family that was in my office recently. Husband and Wife in their mid to late twenties, Sticky Horror and Infant Monster, perhaps five and two respectively. They had been touring the South Coast looking at second-hand sailing yachts and, now reeling from the blandishments they had received from of a host of brokers, thought it was time they dropped in on their neighbourhood surveyor for some hard advice.

Coffees in hand, the couple faced me across my desk. Sticky Horror was gazing blankly about, no doubt looking for something to destroy. Infant Monster was amusing itself pulling the leaves off Chele's lovingly nurtured avocado plant. I asked what kind of boat they were looking for, and the conversation continued.

'Oh, we're not fussy. Thirty to forty feet, maybe.'

Wife nodded her agreement. 'We need lots of space, you see — what with the children.'

And I could see. Whilst Chele was distracted restraining Infant Monster, Sticky Horror had managed to sidle over to the computer and was stabbing at the keyboard with chocolate smeared fingers.

I mentioned something about them being a bit of a handful and now both Husband and Wife were nodding vigorously. Outside on the forecourt I could see their modest family car. They were a neatly dressed family, but obviously not wealthy. I asked what sort of sailing they were planning. Husband looked sheepish. Wife looked apprehensive.

'Actually, sort of blue water cruising. Couple of years in the Med. West Indies — that kind of stuff.'

'Eventually,' added Wife.

'Oh, yes, eventually,' agreed Husband with a notable slump in tone.

'After we've learned how to do it,' said Wife, sensing a slight advantage.

Husband giggled nervously. 'Well, of course, dearest. That goes without saying.' He leaned forward. 'I used to crew for a friend some years ago.'

'But that was only a dinghy,' said Wife.

Husband rolled his eyes heavenwards. His tone became pained. 'Yes, I know it was, darling — but the principles are just the same. And there have been the evening classes...'

'Coastal Skipper,' pressed on Wife, with heavy emphasis on the first word.

'But we wouldn't be sailing alone — that's what we agreed.' Husband turned to me. 'We thought perhaps another couple. That's another reason why we need a fairly large boat. Maybe a centre cockpit. Privacy, you see...'

Wife folded her hands primly in her lap. Chele shot me a glance. Sailing for any length of time in mixed company teaches you that such modesty is impossible. There are few bodily secrets amongst the crew of a small boat. But I could definitely see their point about the children.

'And of course a separate cabin for the kids,' said Wife, almost echoing my thoughts. 'How much do you think we'll need to spend?'

I told her, and her eyes widened. Perhaps a little beyond their reach, I suggested gently. Wife readily agreed. A figure was mentioned. Even the difference in cost between a thirty footer (9.14m) and a forty footer

(12.19m) seemed likely to exceed the total amount they had at their disposal. And I doubted if they had yet considered the running costs.

Husband was talking again. 'One plan was to look for an old boat which we could do up over the winter. You know the sort of thing — structurally okay but a bit tatty.'

'But you're all fingers and thumbs,' accused Wife. 'And I've been waiting for that kitchen shelf for ages.'

As much to defuse the fermenting marital storm, I took them outside into the adjacent boatyard. Five minutes later we were standing before an elderly carvel planked yacht, once jaunty, now downright decrepit. It was about forty feet (12.19m) long, and for sale within their price range. I had obtained the keys from the broker. We climbed aboard.

'I suppose,' said Husband, poking doubtfully at a soft patch in the cabin side, 'we could get a shipwright in to do the more difficult jobs.'

Wife was fingering the mouldering upholstery with distaste. Sticky Horror had pulled the dipstick out of the engine and was offering it to Infant Monster to suck.

Good shipwrights don't come cheap, so it seemed an appropriate moment to quote typical hourly rates. Jaws dropped. Husband's mental apparatus started clicking away, almost audibly.

'It'd cost a fortune,' he admitted at last, and ventured an estimate. I suggested he doubled it to be on the safe side. His expression became glummer. Wife looked stunned.

Back in the office, we sought to distil the reality from the dream. It had become quite evident to me that there was a yawning disparity between their ambitions and their means. Even stretching things a bit, it seemed that their funds would only just run to the purchase of a fairly basic second-hand family cruising yacht, somewhere around the twenty-four foot (7.31m) mark. It was also obvious that their lack of experience (let alone their parental responsibilities to Sticky Horror and Infant Monster) would restrict them to inland and coastal passages for at least the next few seasons. Husband, I learned, had a job in the Midlands and surely couldn't devote the time required to shuttle back and forth to the South Coast in order to restore an old boat.

I thought that at heart they were a practical couple. Hopefully, it was dawning upon them that, whilst their dreams were flexible, their supply of cash and their other personal circumstances were not. A modest boat, easily handled and not too expensive, would suit them far better. Without too much pain it could provide them with immense enjoyment and the experience they needed until they were ready to move on to grander things.

But Wife still had consternation writ large on her brow. 'Separate cabins,' she said suddenly, breaking the expectant hush. 'I'm sorry, I don't want to sound unreasonable, but I insist. A separate cabin for us, one for the boys, and another for guests — all with standing headroom. Oh, and a good sized galley and an enclosed loo.'

I blinked. Were we still talking twenty-four footers?

'I saw this boat at Earl's Court,' she continued, no doubt with memories of the potted plants and piped music swimming in her head, 'that had so much space you wouldn't believe it.' And she went on to name a class of yacht. I felt a little crest-fallen. Until then I was sure we were heading in the right direction. But Wife had obviously been seduced by those ingenious exponents of the quart-into-a-pint-pot school of yacht design. You only have to look at some of the advertisements in the yachting magazines to see evidence of their work. Lush photographs and screaming hyperbole. 'Thirty foot of uncompromising luxury! Three double staterooms, all with *en suite* toilets! Room to seat twenty guests! Hot running water! Central heating! The comforts of home at sea!' — you know the kind of thing.

And, sadly, this is powerful stuff. Boatbuilders have learned that nothing sells like accommodation. The more berths you can cram into a boat, the greater will be its attraction. On a larger yacht, this may be of little consequence, but it is often the kiss of death for smaller designs. Optimum hull shapes become grossly swollen to provide more volume. Freeboards are raised to increase headroom and to enhance the visual impression of space. The boat, eminently salesworthy but now grotesquely rotund and having the windage of a small barn, is a marvel alongside but a misery at sea. We shall touch on this again later.

Husband and Wife seemed doomed to be disappointed. In the first instance they had wanted too much boat for their money, and, when this proved impossible, they were then demanding too much accommodation for their boat. Either way, they were attempting to make their resources stretch to cover requirements which, although understandably desirable, were quite beyond reasonable reach.

This is, of course, a cautionary tale. But Husband and Wife are the representatives of so many encounters I have had over the years. For, when otherwise sensible people dream of sailing, a sense of realism is often the first casualty. The man toiling to resurrect an unrestorable boat is a familiar sight. Yachts, almost permanently laid up ashore because their owners are hopelessly, and ever-increasingly, in arrears with the bills, can be found clogging every boatyard. In these cases the dream has become a nightmare — a nightmare which might have been avoided had they been realistic in their aims and not succumbed to what is, after all, just a rather romantic form of greed.

Better by far to choose a boat which, firstly, is properly suited to the kind of sailing you *really* plan to do and, secondly, can be bought and maintained without dragging you into penury.

In later pages we will explore the various elements which will help you make your choice. But, in the meantime, it would be helpful to summarise the questions which should be answered.

How much can you afford to spend? This is the crux of the matter — perhaps the most significant factor, which will influence almost every other decision you make. It is also the question that demands the most honesty, for the dream can easily outpace the pocket.

Up front, of course, will be the price of the boat, plus the survey and other fees incurred in its purchase. But that's only the start. Downstream will be all the upkeep and maintenance costs that go with being a boat owner. These will include: marina or mooring charges, insurance, harbour dues, plus a reasonable allowance for repairs and equipment replacement. In a later chapter, we shall go into the matter of costs in greater detail. For now it's sufficient to bear their existence in mind, and to attempt not to underestimate them.

What type of cruising do you intend to do? This can be an awkward question to answer — particularly if you are still feeling your way. It's easy to be over-ambitious at first. To some extent we are all armchair sailors at heart, poring over the cruising yarns whilst the rain pelts down outside. And it makes alluring reading. Not for the writer the short hops down the coast, putting into port nightly for a pint of beer and a pizza. For them it's all azure seas, leaping dolphins, and captivating distant lands. Hardly surprisingly, it's very easy to find it all rather attractive.

But reality can impose different rhythms. Even if we have the skills and experience to go ocean voyaging, many of us are pinned down by day-to-day responsibilities such as parenthood or career obligations. As much as we might wish to take off with nary a care, it is probable that soberer considerations will prevail. It therefore makes no sense to choose a long distance cruiser when, in truth, a comfortable family yacht would suit us better.

Also, consider the physical nature of your chosen cruising ground. If the waters are shallow, then draught will be important. If you intend to moor far up a river, then a powerful engine will help you get in and out. And what about racing? Although your primary intention is to cruise, you may want to compete, on a casual basis at least, and there's no finer way to polish your sailing skills. If so, then a slow, heavy displacement yacht is unlikely to be the right choice for you.

Perhaps the best advice is to think fairly short term. Buy the boat which will suit you best *now.* If and when your requirements change, you can always sell it and look for another.

Where will you keep your boat? Of course, marinas will berth almost anything at a price, but if you plan to leave your sailboat on a drying or shallow water mooring, then a bilge keeler, centre-boarder or a multihull may be your best bet.

Some smaller boats can even be kept at home and trailed back and forth to the water. This is rarely as easily accomplished as the advertisements claim, and can quickly become a chore after the first few launches. But it does offer the possibility of reaching new cruising areas much more quickly than would be possible by sea. Someone I know regularly tows his boat across Europe. In succeeding summers he has cruised the Baltic, Mediterranean, and Adriatic seas, launching his boat in precisely the area he chooses without the slog of having to sail it there first.

How much accommodation do you really need? Some time ago I did a stint at the London Boat Show, on the stand of a well-known builder. I had just showed a man over a mid-size GRP yacht and was encouraged by his general air of approval. I was growing hopeful of clinching the sale. 'Not bad, eh?' I said, slapping the hull in a fondish sort of way. 'Seven berths in a boat of this size.'

The man stiffened, then fixed me with a look that would have stripped varnish. 'Young man,' he growled, 'I don't even *know* six other people I'd want to go sailing with!'

I have come to know exactly what he meant. Sailing can strain relationships more than any other activity I know. I once sailed to Gibraltar with a man who cared to whistle television jingles, all slightly off key. I had known him for years and previously had enjoyed his company. But as we proceeded southwards, and those mindless tunes mingled with the more natural sounds of the sea, my feelings of warmth towards him progressively corroded until, by the end of our first week, I could cheerfully have taken him by the throat and brought him to an early but final cadence. On his part, he was apparently incensed with something equally trivial in my manner, for we ended the trip glowering at each other and, to this day, cannot meet without a mutual shudder of apprehension.

If anything, be modest in your requirements. Most owners I know have difficulty making up their crews, and frequently end up sailing short-handed. Ask any experienced yachtsman and he will tell you that a sensible galley and navigation space is worth any number of unwanted berths.

What type of rig would you prefer? This is a fairly technical question which you should leave until you have read further. Beware the romantic preconceptions. The more-masts-the-merrier approach to rigging can ruin a smaller sized yacht. Simple is usually best.

What material should the boat be built of? Another subject which we will explore more fully in later pages. This again is an area where misconceptions abound. Aesthetic preferences, longevity, cost, maintenance, and the nature of your intended cruising will be the factors that will influence your choice.

There are many ways to go cruising. Fairlight meets Canberra off Palma.

Chapter 3

THE MONOHULL

To the purist, to even admit the necessity of the word *monohull* is a tacit and unwelcome acknowledgement that other types exist. For him a boat with a single hull is simply the only kind of 'boat' — other forms such as 'catamaran' and 'trimaran' (with two and three hulls respectively) being grotesque aberrations, unworthy of mention in the same breath. But, for the purposes of this book, that clearly won't do. The phrase 'a boat' is obviously too vague. To tighten it a little and talk about a 'keelboat' will not improve the situation because this becomes too specific — ignoring, for instance, bilge keelers and centre-boarders which, by our previous prejudiced terms of reference, are also obviously 'boats'.

Therefore I am unrepentant. From here onwards, where there might be ambiguity, boats with only one hull are *monohulls*, and those with more are *multihulls*. A *boat* or a *yacht* can have any number of hulls and still qualify. Hopefully, the sub-species of both monohull and multihull will clearly emerge as we proceed.

The monohull yacht forms the vast majority of those afloat around the world. Their development springs directly from the smaller types of fishing and commercial sailing vessels which have plied the seas for centuries. To this day, in older or 'character' yachts, the lineage is still discernible. But the modern yacht at its best — in the technical sense at least — is a refined and sophisticated sailing machine that owes only a token nod towards the past.

Sailing directly upwind is a feat which, to this day, continues to elude sailors. To make progress to windward, a sailing boat must attempt to **point** at as close an angle to the wind's direction as it can — often following a zig-zag course, which is known as **beating.** Early ships, with their inefficient rigs, were essentially downwind craft — obliged to choose routes where the prevailing winds where favourable. Apart from some notable exceptions, such as Mediterranean feluccas and Arab dhows, they were usually square rigged with only a few fore-and-aft sails, and were incapable of sailing much closer than side-on on to the wind. Even the majestic clippers, still trading at the beginning of this century, could only manage to sail within a measly six points (just under 70 degrees) — a quite lamentable performance by modern standards. With the development of the fore-and-aft rig, great gains in windward efficiency have been achieved. Today's yacht is typically capable of

tacking (altering course through the wind so that it blows on the opposite side of the sails) through 80 degrees (40 degrees each side of the wind's direction), giving it a flexibility of movement quite beyond the scope of our ancestors.

Since Joshua Slocum's first singlehanded circumnavigation of the world, completed in 1898, the monohull has proved itself a firm favourite amongst cruising yachtsmen. And with good reason. If well designed and soundly constructed, its integrated, compact form is ideal for withstanding the onslaught of the sea. A well-bunged barrel will survive even the severest conditions in open water, and the monohull bears some similarity to that ideal. However, the analogy is not completely apt because, eventually, that barrel will be dashed ashore somewhere, perhaps to be destroyed. A boat, on the other hand, must be capable of manoeuvre — not only in fair weather but also in foul. It relies for its safety as much upon its ability to *navigate* as it does upon its buoyancy.

But, of course, not everybody wants to endure the epic stuff. And, if they are sensible, there is no reason why they should. Coastal cruises and short hops across open water can usually be undertaken within the reliable period of weather forecasting — say forty-eight hours. In detail, meteorologists sometimes get it wrong, but their predictions of general weather trends have become increasingly well honed. Today, no one need set off on a short trip unforewarned.

This has an important bearing on choice of boat. The harsher vagaries of the weather can catch an ocean sailor offshore — I've been soundly pummelled on a number of occasions myself — and, should this happen, his boat must be capable of taking whatever might befall. But the coastal cruise can usually be planned to avoid such nasties and, as a consequence, the boat's design can, within reason, be pitched more towards comfort and convenience than an ability to survive ultimate conditions.

Size, too, is an important consideration. To take a twenty-footer (6.09m) to windward in a Force 6 is to know what it is to be swallowed by a cement mixer. But in the same conditions a fifty-footer (15.24m) would be just starting to pick up her heels. Although incredibly long voyages have been made in incredibly small boats, there is an inescapable relationship between what you intend to do and what you intend to do it *in*. Pocket yachts generally mean pocket cruises.

The question of aesthetics is one I don't propose to dwell on. Where boats are concerned, beauty is very much in the eye of the beholder —

and who am I to judge what appeals to anyone other than myself? There is a reasoned argument that if something looks right, it probably is right, but this can be deceptive because, once again, romanticism often blurs our judgement. Be wary of superfluous add-ons and counterfeit traditionalism. A good honest boat can combine efficiency with elegance, without the need for moulded fibreglass figureheads or other cosmetic fripperies.

General Design Considerations:

The design of any sailing boat brings together a complex and subtle brew of interacting factors. Boats live in the ever-moving interface between sea and sky — in both a hydro-dynamic and an aerodynamic environment, each of which imposes its special disciplines and limitations. Yacht designers struggle to wring the maximum benefit from both.

It would be beyond the scope of this book to delve too deeply into all the intricacies involved, but it is important that yachtsmen have some grasp of the basic principles so that, by simply examining any boat, they can assess its general characteristics and decide whether or not it is the kind of boat for them.

Apart from the domestic arrangements — which we shall cover in a later chapter — the most vivid evidence of the designer's skill (or lack of it) will show in the yacht's *performance* and *handling characteristics.*

By performance we mean boat speed, good or bad for the size of boat. In some cruising circles 'performance' — which by implication we can take as meaning *high* performance — is a dirty word, only of interest to the racing community, of whom of course we should thoroughly disapprove.

In my opinion this is an absurdity. There is no particular merit in lumbering around at four knots when you could be doing five. The difference in speed could shave three hours off a cross Channel jaunt and five days off a trade wind crossing of the Atlantic. A very experienced friend of mine once attempted to deliver a traditional wooden cruising yacht from England, via the West Indies, to Annapolis, Maryland. It was a vessel of awesome weight and lethargic turn of speed. He allowed what he thought would be ample time but, in the event, the voyage took so long he got frozen into the Intercoastal Waterway somewhere south of the Chesapeake Bay, and had to return in the following spring to continue his journey. The notion that cruising boats should be slow boats is a nonsense. Boats which sail well are efficient boats and, apart from being faster, are usually more pleasurable and less exhausting to sail.

The main factors that influence performance are as follows:

Displacement: In common with all floating objects, boats comply with Archimedes Principle, namely that they displace a quantity of water equal to their own mass (and for our purposes we can consider 'mass' to mean 'weight'). This weight is known as the **displacement weight** or, more simply, the **displacement** which can be expressed in pounds, kilograms, or tons. It represents the actual weight of the vessel whereas other apparent forms of tonnage — Thames (now virtually extinct) and Registered Tonnage — result from arcane formulae derived from volume or the number of 'tuns' (casks) of wine a boat can carry. Few of us would fail to be intrigued by the social implications of the latter, but it's hardly a lot of help when judging weight.

As a sailboat is basically just a machine which harnesses a source of power (the wind) to create movement against restraining influences (weight and drag), it also conforms with the general principles of power/weight ratio — the heavier the boat, the greater power will be required to propel it. We will touch on this later in this chapter but, for the moment, it can be accepted that the heavier the boat, the slower it is likely to be.

Waterline Length: Often abbreviated as **LWL.** This is really self-explanatory, being the distance between the points at which the stem and stern of the vessel emerge from the water. Waterline length limits the top speed of any *displacement* craft (as opposed to **planing** type craft such as speedboats and sailing dinghies).

This limitation is caused by the way the hull generates waves as it moves through the water. The faster the boat moves, the greater the distance (wave length) between the peaks of these waves. Figure 1 shows the vessel moving slowly. A bow wave has been formed, and smaller waves are being developed towards the stern. As the boat speed increases, so does the wave length. Figure 2 shows the vessel sailing at top speed. The wave length now approximates to the boat's LWL, with the boat supported horizontally by its bow and stern wave. Because the fattest and most buoyant portion of the boat hangs over the trough, it has already sunk lower into the water. And, finally, Figure 3 shows the

Fig 1. The yacht sailing at less than hull speed

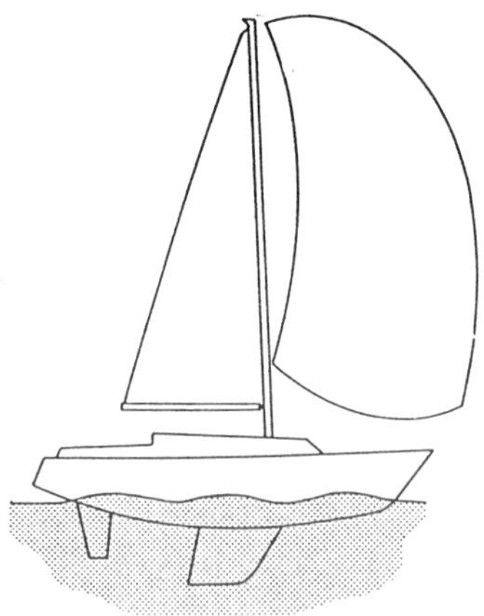

Fig 2. At hull speed. The wave length equals LWL.

Fig 3. Attempting to sail faster than hull speed. The yacht must sail uphill over its own bow wave.

vessel attempting to sail faster than this. The wave length has increased beyond LWL., the boat's stern has dropped into the trough, and the boat is now presented with the daunting task of sailing uphill over its own bow wave. This obviously calls for a colossal amount of extra power, more than the sails can realistically provide. So, for all practical purposes, the situation as shown in Figure 2 is the maximum speed attainable and is commonly known as the **hull speed.**

Hull speed can be calculated by multiplying the square root of LWL in feet by 1.34 (or the square root of LWL in metres by 2.43). If you apply this formula to various boats, you will see that top speeds rise markedly with waterline length. For instance a boat of 25' (7.62m) LWL can achieve just under 7 knots, and one of 50' (15.24m) LWL just over 9 knots. In the case of very lightweight craft, these speeds can be exceeded in ideal conditions, as they can at least partially plane along the surface. However, for most practical purposes, hull speed can usually be regarded as the maximum.

Before we move on, it is worth noting that we can relate displacement and length in a way that allows us to compare boats of different sizes. To talk of weight in absolute terms is meaningless. Ten tons would be monstrously heavy for a thirty-two footer but feather light for a boat of fifty feet. What we need to know is exactly what is meant by 'light' or 'heavy' for a boat of any length, and such an indication is given by a useful arithmetical device known as the **displacement/length ratio.** This is reached by a fairly simple formula, namely:

$$\text{D/L Ratio} = \frac{\text{DT}}{(0.01 \times \text{WL})^3}$$

Where DT = Displacement in tons (of 2240 lbs.)
and WL = Waterline Length in feet.

The figures derived from this formula will give a good indication of the relative heaviness of any boat. D/L ratios of around 100 would be ultra-light; 200 would still be considered light; by 300 we are getting into the medium displacement range; and around the 450 mark and beyond you may be thinking of wintering in an ice pack. Generally speaking, the less the D/L ratio, the better the performance, but be wary of a possible trap. The *actual* D/L ratio is obviously dependant upon the *true* weight of the boat at any given time — including all the extra gear you might have put aboard. To load a ton of stores onto a large yacht will have only a marginal affect upon its D/L ratio because it adds only a relatively small proportion of the total displacement. But load the same amount onto a small cruiser and the D/L ratio will soar.

Wetted Surface Area: This is the area of the hull actually in contact with the water, including all appendages such as keels and rudders. As a yacht moves forward, there is considerable friction between the hull surface and the water, creating what is often called **skin drag.** This is the major drag component at very low boat speeds, but diminishes to only about 10% of the total resistance as hull speed is reached and wave drag becomes dominant. It follows that the effect of high wetted surface area is most pronounced in light airs — glued to the water, as the expression so aptly goes. As a surprisingly high percentage of all sailing takes place in wind strengths below that required to achieve hull speed, it's unfortunate that so many designs are unnecessarily extravagant with wetted surface area.

Fairlight, *a Laurent-Giles designed cutter built in Devon in 1938. Although very much a yacht, her links with the past are quite apparent.*

Sail Area: Sails are the power-house of the sailboat, and it should come as no surprise to learn that the larger the area that can be set, the more power you have available to overcome resistance in its various forms. Sail areas are, of course, variable. We increase and reduce sail to suit the current weather conditions. This variability can cause confusion when comparing boats, as designers and builders can choose different parameters when declaring it. Some will take the area of the mainsail and the working jib, others the mainsail and the largest headsail, and so on. The most usual method — and the one we shall use — is the area of the mainsail plus the area of the foretriangle contained between the mast, the forestay, and the distance between the foot of the mast and the point where the forestay emerges from the deck, as shown by the shaded area in Figure 4.

Nothing reveals a boat's intent more clearly than the sail plan. A lofty, spindly, flexible rig proclaims a racing boat; a shorter, simpler, more robust arrangement spells cruising. Within reason the sail area should be generous — it's always possible to reduce sail but impossible to increase it beyond that which the rig will allow. Designers can be rather timid in this regard, and their boats are often woefully under-canvassed for light conditions or for use in areas where light winds predominate, such as the Mediterranean and much of the United States coast.

Again we have a simple formula which will allow us to assess the relationship between the power available (sail area) and the weight to be moved (displacement), and also to provide comparison between boats of different sizes. The figure produced is called the **Sail Area/Displacement Ratio** and is arrived at as follows:

$$\text{SA/D Ratio} = \frac{\text{SA}}{(\text{D}/64)^{2/3}}$$

Where SA = Sail area (in square feet)
and D = Displacement (in pounds).

Most boats will be found to have a SA/D ratio between 14 and 20, with the higher figure indicating the more powerful end of the range. A typical medium displacement cruiser with an ample, but not ridiculously excessive rig, would be likely to turn in a SA/D ratio of about 17 or 18.

So, before we move on to the design considerations that affect stability and handling, let's recap on performance and offer some cautionary

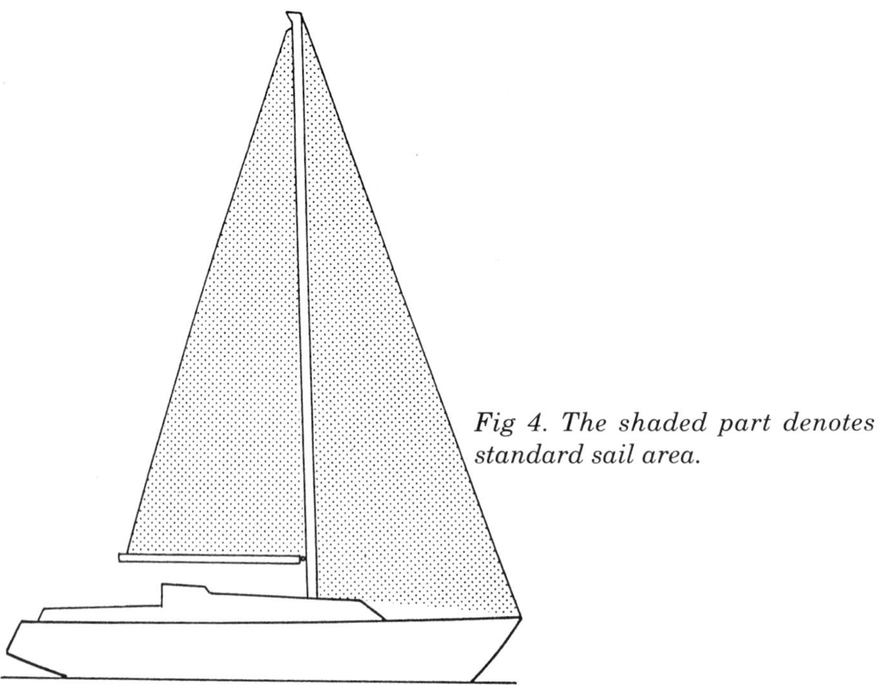

Fig 4. The shaded part denotes standard sail area.

qualifications. Expressed very crudely: heavy displacement, short waterline length, large wetted surface area, and meagre sail area are slow; light displacement, long waterline length, low wetted surface area, and generous sail area are fast. But already I feel the risks in such generalisation, can sense the critics reaching for their pens, the exceptions buzzing through their minds. For instance, a heavy displacement and high sail area boat can be faster in light conditions because it may have a relatively low wetted surface area for its weight. A boat with a low sail area may not be disadvantaged in heavy weather because other boats will have been forced to **reef** (reduce sail). Similarly, high sail area can become superfluous (even dangerous) beyond the point where maximum speed is reached. Different types of boats prosper in different conditions. There is no such thing as the universal design, perfect in every situation. The ideal cruising sailboat looks for versatility in performance over the widest range of possible conditions.

But performance isn't everything. Fast is nice but so is *comfortable* — and we're not talking of the thickness of the cushions here. It's not just the ease with which a boat moves through the water that's important, but also the manner. Some yachts are cranky and exhausting to sail, others are a pleasure. The word *seakindly* describes the well-mannered boat perfectly, the words for the contrary type are numerous and often unprintable.

The ability of a sailboat to resist the heeling effect of the sails is termed its **stability.** A very stable boat is called a **stiff** boat, and one less stable is described as **tender.**

Stability is achieved in two ways: Firstly, by the shape of the hull — known as **form stability** — and secondly by attaching a heavy lead or iron **ballast keel** to pull the boat upright as it heels over. The wider the hull, the more stable the boat. The more ballast there is, or the deeper it is carried, the more righting effect it provides.

The way in which these variable options are applied is one of the thorniest the yacht designer faces. Lighter boats — which by definition obviously cannot carry too much ballast otherwise they would be heavier — must look towards beam to supply much of their stability. Very narrow boats, with less form stability, must carry more ballast to compensate and are, as a consequence, heavier. From the cruising yacht standpoint, these trade-offs are significant. There is a powerful inducement for commercial boatbuilders to construct their boats as light as is practicable, because less material is used, hence less cost. At first this wouldn't seem too much of a problem so long as the boat remains structurally adequate — lighter is faster, after all. But, unfortunately, these necessarily beamy boats can be very strenuous to steer and can also be uncomfortable when pounding to windward in a lumpy sea.

So, our yacht designer, being a sailor himself and no stranger to discomfort, now opts for a soft life and moderate beam and is confronted with another choice. He can bolt on more ballast and make the boat heavier, or he can still go for lightish displacement by placing the ballast *deeper.* But of course now there may be an unacceptable price to pay in terms of increased **draught.**

Where stability is concerned there is, as you can see, a triangular relationship between displacement, beam and draught. Whichever way you play it, you lose something, and sometimes you lose a lot.

For there is another important factor — weight aloft. Later we shall deal with various sail handling devices and other items which can place extra weight high in the rig. Sufficient to say for now that small boats can be seriously put at risk by injudiciously adding weight where it can detrimentally affect the stability.

Directional stability should not be confused with anything to do with heeling. This phrase covers the ability of a boat to hold its course. A directionally stable boat will require less attention from the helmsman to maintain its heading — indeed, many such boats, if properly trimmed, will sail for hours or even days unattended. A directionally *unstable* boat, on the other hand, will tend to wander, needing always a correcting hand to keep it on course. Keel and rudder design are the main affecting influences here. Usually, the proportionately longer the keel, the more directionally stable the boat. But, this again is an area where skill in design will show.

Yacht designing is very much the art of compromise. The various design considerations can be blended in an infinite number of ways — each providing subtle differences in performance and handling characteristics. It is up to the designer to make this blend as intelligently as he can to satisfy the functional requirements of the type of boat he is designing. And it is up to the buyer to attempt to interpret these differences, and to choose which particular cocktail suits him best.

Spook, *designed and built by the author, is a thoroughly modern cruising keelboat.*

Chapter 4

THE KEELBOAT

Mention the word 'yacht' and the keelboat springs to mind. It is the archetype of the species. A monohull with a single ballasted keel mounted underneath on the centre-line, it is the classic yachty shape.

And yet some of the most modern examples are far from classic in concept, stretching as they do into the outer reaches of hydrodynamic knowledge. Weirdly shaped wing keels can be seen appended to equally weirdly bulging hulls — all trying to squeeze an extra fraction of a knot from that ultimate limitation, hull speed, or to gain some advantage from a complicated racing rule.

But, generally speaking, the cruising keelboat is a far less complex beast — indeed, this is its supreme advantage. From the structural standpoint, it approaches the ideal — an egg-like capsule of immense strength. Often, especially in older designs, the hull is entirely monocoque, with the keel an integrated extension of the whole. Sometimes the ballast is totally encapsulated within the envelope of the hull's skin, eliminating the possibility of leakage around bolts. But, more often these days, the keel is a casting of lead or iron, simply bolted externally to the underside of the hull. This arrangement, though more vulnerable and potentially troublesome than the encapsulated keel, lends itself well to modern production techniques, and allows the manufacturer to offer variations on the same hull theme — a fin keeled and bilge keeled version from the same mould, for example.

The most significant disadvantage of the keelboat is its draught. Typically, a 30 footer (9.14m) will draw about 5' 3" (1.60m), a comparable bilge keeler 3' 9" (1.14m), and a centre-boarder perhaps as little as 2' 6" (0.76m) with its board raised. In tidal or shallow waters, this could be crucial to your choice. For long distance cruising offshore, it's of little importance.

Evolving as it has from traditional working boats, the keelboat has been around long enough to develop several sub-types. It would be useful to look at these individually, so, the characteristics of three representative types are described below.

Traditional, long keeled type: Almost certainly of heavy displacement. This type has a high wetted surface area which, combined with its displacement, makes it likely to be slow in light and moderate winds. They excel in heavy conditions but are inclined to be 'wet', taking a lot of water on deck as they plough through the waves, rather than riding over them. However, their motion in these conditions is often more comfortable than that of lighter displacement boats. Long keeled yachts often have very good directional stability, and can be left, sometimes for many hours, to steer themselves without anyone at the helm. Handling can be hard work. Heavy displacement calls for larger than average sail areas which sometimes — because of the traditional nature of such boats — have to be managed with simple, some would say crude, equipment. Under engine power — especially when going astern — they can be very awkward to manoeuvre.

This type is for those who place comfort above speed. Being generally rather ponderous boats, they are, perhaps, better suited to middle to long distance cruising rather than the casual afternoon trip. Devotees of this type are often disdainful of more sprightly boats — perhaps a mistake, because in cruising there is considerable advantage in getting to places quickly.

A very heavy displacement, long keeled ketch.

Very light displacement, fin keeled type: The opposite extreme, derived from pure racing craft. The fin keels are frequently rather narrow in the fore-and-aft dimension (termed **high aspect ratio** keels) to minimise wetted surface area and to optimise other hydrodynamic considerations. Often, these boats have a cantilevered spade rudder, not supported by a skeg. This type of boat is obviously very buoyant, sometimes having a rather twitchy motion in choppy conditions, and tending to pound badly when beating to windward. However, they are notably fast in all but the heaviest conditions (where their lightness makes it difficult to drive them through the waves). They can often exceed their hull speed by planing like dinghies.

Stability is usually gained by wide beam, making them spacious below but often very heavy to steer when heeled over more than a few degrees. Directional stability is usually poor, particularly downwind in rough conditions when they tend to slew from side to side. Control under engine power is usually very good, with extremely tight turning circles that make them highly manoeuvrable in marinas.

High performance sailboats are demanding to sail. Their rigs and sail plans can often be complicated, requiring constant 'tuning' to get the best out of them. Because of the limitations on weight, construction of the hull and equipment tends to be pared to the minimum, making them rather fragile.

These boats are for those who would like to race or who would like a lot of excitement with their cruising. Their speed brings more distant destinations closer — no bad thing. But this is not a relaxing way to sail.

Scarlet Oyster, *a Lightwave 48 class sloop, designed by Carl Schumacher. A light displacement, fast cruising yacht with racing potential.*

Moderate displacement, fin and skeg type: This type commands the middle ground of cruising keelboats and there is a great variety of choice in the specifics of each design. Although the rudder is not always skeg hung, it commonly is, giving better structural support and improving directional stability. As this type represents a compromise between the extremes, so its performance and handling characteristics stand somewhere between the sluggishness of the heavy displacement boat and the dazzling speed and twitchiness of the light. Beam can be narrow, or moderate, depending on the nature of the design and the accommodation and load-carrying requirements. Comfort at sea varies very much according to the designer's skill, but it is nearly always better than the very light displacement boat. Handling under engine power is also very variable — some are very good and some downright awful. Sails tend to be fairly easy to handle. Many boats of this type use roller furling. Of all keelboat types, this is probably the most versatile. Unless there are compelling reasons to the contrary, a boat within this group would probably be the first choice for most cruising yachtsmen. In size, quality, and cost, there is a huge selection to choose from.

A Sadler 32 — a typical medium displacement fin and skeg yacht.

Chapter 5

THE BILGE KEELER

The **bilge keeler** or **twin keel** yacht is a relative newcomer to the sailing scene. In 1924 the Hon. R. A.Balfour built a 23 foot sloop called *Bluebird* and cruised it extensively. Instead of a single central keel, this boat had a pair of parallel keels protruding from its bilge, and could sail in waters too shallow to admit more traditional craft.

But it was not until the late forties that the idea really took hold, and even then it was mainly in Britain. For the bilge keeler has always been a curiously British phenomena and its chief exponent, the designer Robert Tucker, was almost single-handededly responsible for its popularity. Thousands of people, eager to shrug off the grim memories of the war, were introduced to the joys of sailing in simple and affordable boats, usually built of plywood and built in vast numbers. I was one of them, and I recall those days very fondly.

Early designs had short, stubby keels, sometimes made asymmetric in shape in the belief that this produced useful hydro-dynamic lift to windward. Other boats carried the ballast on the centre line, the keels themselves simply being steel plates. Neither of these arrangements proved effective in resisting **leeway** (the tendency of a sailboat to slide sideways, described more fully in the next chapter) and were soon rejected by designers. Modern bilge keelers favour deeper, symmetrical keels which, although more efficient, have given away some of the advantage of shallower draught. Typically, a modern bilge keeler will draw about 1' 6" (0.48m) less than its fin keeled counterpart.

The other advantage offered by bilge keelers is that they can **take the ground** without toppling over when the tide recedes — an obvious boon if the boat is to be kept on a tidal mooring or should you want to beach it for scrubbing off or any other reason. A word of warning, however: should a bilge keeler accidentally run aground, it's usually stuck there until the tide lifts it off. A keelboat can often be freed by heeling it to reduce the draught.

Of course every arrangement has its debit side and the bilge keeler is no exception. The main criticisms relate to performance, which is not quite as good as the equivalent keelboat. This is due to a number of reasons which are easily understood. Firstly, as the ballast is divided between two keels, the combined wetted surface area of both bilge keels is greater, and the low speed performance is impaired. Secondly, there may be an increase in turbulence and some interaction between the keels. These effects are likely to be most apparent when beating to windward — a point of sailing on which certain bilge keelers (especially older designs) have gained some notoriety.

There may also be a disadvantageous affect upon stability. Because of the reduced draught, the ballast is carried higher, and its righting effect is less. In boats identical except for their keel arrangements, the keelboat is often perceptibly stiffer.

There are other disadvantages which are less obvious. Bilge keelers are more prone to structural damage, particularly if kept bouncing up and down on a drying mooring. As the keels are usually inclined outwards, they are subjected to considerable flexural stresses as the weight of the boat comes on them. Settling down onto soft mud will literally wedge the keels apart as the boat sinks lower. Watch a yacht surveyor dive first into the cabin lockers to check the fastenings, and you know he's seen them wrenched out before. Propellers and shafts are also more susceptible. They live in the water flow between the keels — perfectly placed to catch any piece of flotsam drawn down between them.

But is has to be said that, despite the marginal losses in performance and the increased structural vulnerability, the bilge keeler could still remain a viable choice for some. The convenience of shallower draught and beaching ability may well outweigh the small sacrifices in speed and robustness.

A Sadler 26 demonstrates her ability to comfortably take the ground at low tide.

Chapter 6

THE CENTREBOARDER

The ultimate shoal draught monohull is the centre-boarder. If your main requirement is an ability to sail in knee-deep water then this commonly available type could be your choice. Some, goes the joke, draw so little they'll float in damp grass.

Centre-boarders have been around for many years, and were a logical development of **leeboard** (lowerable boards which pivot on the outside of the hull) craft such as the Dutch *botter* and the American sharpie. Unlike bilge-keelers, which are rarely seen larger than 35' (10.67m) LOA, centre-boarders come in all sizes, from tiny day boats up to ocean going monsters.

If they are not to be too tender, centre-boarders need to be fairly beamy boats, having lots of form stability. Ballast is carried, either internally or in the form of a vestigial external keel, with a plate (usually of metal but sometimes of wood or GRP) which can be lowered to resist leeway. Often this plate is a massive iron casting which provides a good proportion — or in some cases all — of the ballast.

This ability to raise and lower the keel at will makes the centre-boarder almost unique amongst monohulls, in that it can reduce its wetted surface area when circumstances permit. In very light conditions or when sailing downwind, up comes the board and down goes the drag.

But, again, there are drawbacks. The inherent complexity of the arrangement makes the type more expensive to build than similar keelboats, and there is likely to be an increase in mechanical problems and associated maintenance. Inside the boat, the centre-board casing encroaches into the accommodation, reducing the space available and providing an obstacle that must be 'designed around'. Interior lay-outs can become rather eccentric as the yacht designer struggles to minimise the intrusion. And many centre-boarders are very noisy; the board bangs against the casing, especially at anchor when there is no sideways load to press it one way or the other.

There is also another potential hazard associated with centre-boarders where the board itself provides a high proportion of the ballast. Should the boat be rolled by a heavy sea, the board may drop into its retracted position (unless positively locked down, a rare facility) and, thereafter, will provide only a very reduced righting moment to turn the yacht back upright again. Worse still, the whole installation may not be designed to take severe loads in the inverted position, and the board could cause damage as it crashes down — perhaps even bursting through the top of its casing and out through the deck!

Less dangerous but extremely infuriating: When taking the ground, it's possible for a rock to get jammed in the slot, making it impossible to lower the board when you get back out into deeper water. I've known of very heavy centreboards being locked up by ridiculously small pebbles, and recall, with no great pleasure, once having to dive under a boat to prise one loose.

Chapter 7
THE MULTIHULL

There are many different types of multihull, but the two that have been adopted and developed by western designers are the **catamaran** (the word comes from the Tamil *kattu-maram,* meaning 'tied wood') and the **trimaran.** The catamaran has two hulls, joined by cross beams or a central cabin structure, and the trimaran has three.

Historically, the multihull springs from the Indian Ocean and Pacific regions, and has a heritage dating back into antiquity. Originally they were very narrow canoes, stabilised by either lashing two hulls side-by-side, or by fitting outriggers to a single hull on one or both sides depending on type. Many remarkable voyages were made in these craft. The Polynesian double canoe, for example, was used as a method of transport for colonisation, having a raised central platform on which living quarters were built to house those early colonists. It was in these simple boats that man spread from the Malay peninsular and Indonesia, through the Pacific islands, right down to New Zealand.

The western affair with multihulls goes back a fair time. In 1663 a gentleman by the name of Sir William Petty designed and built the spritsail-rigged catamaran *Simon and Jude.* And over two hundred years later no less a person than the renowned American yacht designer, Captain Nathaniel Herreshoff had a brief flirtation with the type. The year was 1876, and the onlookers at the Centennial Regatta in New York harbour were chagrined to see his 25 foot catamaran, *Amaryllis*, trounce the more conventional opposition. One might have supposed that the esteem Herreshoff was held in would have invested his boat with instant respectability. Unfortunately, this was not to be, for such was the general indignation at his boldness, our innovative Captain was pointedly discouraged from further competition. As if to rub it in, he apparently took to chasing the steamers out to sea instead.

The perception of the multihull as a freakish device has been an enduring prejudice to this day. After Herreshoff, development stagnated for about seventy years. It was not until after the Second World War that interest really took root, and the struggle towards some sort of sensible recognition began. F. H."Skip" Creger started building catamarans in California, and in England the brothers Roland and Francis Prout were developing their famous double-hulled dinghy, the *Shearwater*. By the late fifties another Californian, Arthur Piver, was designing a range of plywood trimarans, and other designers and builders (myself included) were sharpening their pencils.

The main qualities offered by the multihull are speed, accommodation, stability, and shallow draught. To a great extent the first two are inversely proportional — the more living space you go for, the less performance, and vice-versa. It was unfortunate for the development of the type that, when it first emerged on the yachting scene, some designers (with the instincts of slum landlords) gazed at the cavernous interiors, knowing that nothing appealed more potently to the gullible than a large number of berths. Slim, light hulls can be blisteringly fast; add weight and space, and the hulls become fatter, with an attendant loss of speed. The notion that every multihull is faster than a monohull of similar length is fallacious. The best certainly are, but the worst can be absolute plodders.

Multihulls generate waves in the same manner as any other boat, but these waves are less pronounced. The fine hulls and light weight of the multihull allow it more easily to transcend the usual barrier of hull speed. But be sceptical of the many preposterous claims that abound. Although amazing top speeds are possible, as a rule most multihulls are no more than 20% faster than a comparable monohull over an extended course. As an example, I averaged just over 6 knots from England to Texas in a 35 foot racing trimaran that could touch 20 knots in ideal conditions. In a 35 foot monohull, I might reasonably have expected to average 5 knots over the same voyage.

And in some circumstances multihulls can even be slower. Many have a large wetted surface area and are very sluggish in light conditions.

Others carry so much **top hamper** (structure above the waterline) that they are acutely punished when attempting to sail to windward. They can also be slow to **go about** (change tack from the wind on one bow to the wind on the other) and difficult to handle when under power.

The Achilles heel of the multihull is capsize. As they carry no ballast and are entirely reliant upon their beam to provide stability, they are just as stable (indeed, often more so) upside down as they are the right way up. Beam and weight and a properly matched sail area are the determining factors. Form stability increases by the power of four, so if you double the size of a multihull the stability increases by sixteen times ($2^4 = 16$). So far as stability is concerned, big is beautiful. However, multihull sailors are quick to point out that, although it's true that their boats can capsize, they are likely to remain afloat and will still support the crew. Would you, they ask, prefer to be on a sinking keelboat? They have a point.

But perhaps the main disadvantage of owning a multihull is the unsympathetic treatment dished out by marina operators. Nearly all marinas are designed to take keelboats — narrow and deep rather than wide and shallow — and, although it is sometimes possible to find space at the end of a pontoon, more often the berthing master will turn you away. This may not be a problem if you plan to keep your boat on a swinging mooring, and to anchor out when cruising, but if the conviviality of marina life is to your taste, then maybe it would be wise to think again. Who knows, perhaps someone will some day wake up to the idea that shallow waters could be profitably developed to accommodate multihulls.

As in all things, there is good and bad with most shades in between. The world of multihulls is populated by some of the dottiest (and most delightful) characters in sailing. The best designers and builders are highly professional and their boats are both exhilarating and safe to sail. The worst aren't.

And now let's move on to consider the two most common types.

Chapter 8

THE CATAMARAN

Despite the inconvenience of wide beam, it would seem at first thought that the combined attractions of good performance, shallow draught, and spacious accommodation would be overwhelming. Everyone should sail catamarans, say the devotees — the perfect yacht — and they would go on to tell you that in a right-thinking world a monohull would be thought of as half a catamaran, and a trimaran as a catamaran and a half.

Cruising catamarans (often abbreviated to 'cats') fall broadly into two types: By far the most common have a central saloon, forming the bridge-deck between the two hulls. Others, usually the smaller classes, restrict the accommodation to the hulls themselves, with an open decking or trampoline between.

The accommodation in the first type is usually very generous for any given length, and can be conveniently divided to provide a high degree of privacy. If, however, this potential for accommodation is over-exploited, then a heavy price will be paid in loss of boat speed.

Multihulls in general, and catamarans in particular, have a reputation for poor windward performance — especially in heavier conditions. This is often exaggerated by their critics but there is some justification for the criticism. The problem lies mainly in the large areas of hull and superstructure above the waterline, exposed to the force of the wind. This area is aptly referred to as **windage** and, with their two hulls and prominent central cabins, catamarans tend to have a lot of it.

Now, the pressure of the wind on vertical surfaces increases with the *square* of the wind velocity, and can be calculated by using Martin's Formula:

$$P = .004V^2$$

Where:

P = Pressure in pounds per square foot.
V = Wind velocity in statute miles per hour.

Spacious accommodation is sometimes achieved at the expense of windage.

Taking a panel of only 10 ft^2 (0.93m^2) as an example we can see that at wind speeds of 10 mph the pressure on that panel will be 4 lbs, at 30 mph it will be 36 lbs, and in a hurricane blowing at 80 mph it will be a staggering 256 lbs (expressed metrically, these pressures on the same panel would be 1.8 kg, 16.3 kg, and 116.1 kg respectively). And this is just for a panel with less area than the average front door! Think about the windage on a typical cruising catamaran and you can easily imagine how awesome the wind pressure could be.

And, whilst dwelling on this, it's worth remembering that boats can **reef** (reduce) their sails to suit the weather conditions, but have to live with their windage come what may. There will come a point where the upwind drive from a reduced sail area will be inadequate to overcome the windage, and *any* boat — but first the catamaran — will find it impossible to proceed.

If a catamaran is to be both efficient and safe it is important that windage be carefully considered at the design stage. Once again a dilemma arises. In order to minimise the prominence of the cabin structure, whilst still retaining reasonable headroom within it, designers are sometimes tempted to lower the bridge-deck, thus reducing the clearance between it and the water. In rough seas, the pounding of the waves against too low a bridge-deck can be extremely uncomfortable. On a catamaran I once misguidedly offered to deliver to the Mediterranean, the bow waves from each hull would literally pile up under the boat, a seething wall of water preventing any further speed increase. The overall performance was so pitiful, it took me five weeks to persuade this horrible craft to sail from Poole to Fuengirola, Spain. On another boat I inspected in my role as surveyor, the bridge-deck had taken so much punishment that a panel had been stove in, scooping up enough water to flood both hulls.

Some catamarans may make excessive **leeway.** As mentioned previously, this is the tendency of a boat to slide a little sideways as it moves forward, and is obviously always in a direction a few degrees downwind of the theoretical course. In exaggerated form, the phenomena is illustrated in Figure 5. All boats make some leeway but catamarans are particularly susceptible. Most use some means to increase the **lateral area** (side view area of the hull below the waterline) to help increase their 'grip' on the water, thus reducing leeway. This may either be fixed keels, or drop boards, hinged or sliding up and down in slots in the hulls. Be wary of claims that some cats can resist leeway without such devices — they can't, or at least not well.

A few people find the motion of a catamaran uncomfortable. Although having enormous initial stability and sailing almost upright, their response to wave motion can be jerky, quite unlike the easy roll and plunge of a keelboat. Try it before you choose. It affects some stomachs but not others.

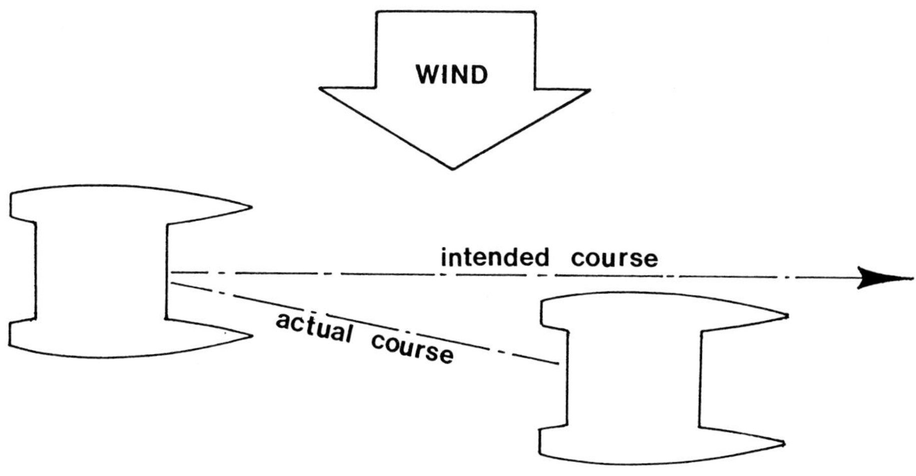

Chapter 9

THE TRIMARAN

This close cousin of the catamaran was a strong runner in the early development of cruising multihulls, but has recently rather faded in popularity.

The reasons for this are various: Structural complexity makes the trimaran a comparatively expensive boat to build. Length for length, the overall beam is invariably greater than a catamaran's (one of my own tris, the 35 ft (10.67m) LOA *Whisky Jack* was a daunting 25 ft (7.62m) wide), although some designs attempt to overcome this problem by contriving to have the **amas** (outer hulls or 'floats') fold inboard, either for transportation or even for berthing alongside. Obviously, the mechanisms needed to provide this facility add still further to the cost.

But in a market greedy for living space, the trimaran suffers by comparison. In all but the largest boats, accommodation is limited to the centre hull, and is typically less than can be provided by a comparable catamaran. From a sales standpoint, these defects are compelling. The trimaran has always been a difficult beast to promote, and boatbuilders have consequently become discouraged.

For the cruising multihull sailor this is rather a pity, for the trimaran does offer some significant technical advantages. Namely: Because it lacks a high bridge-deck structure windage is usually less. Headroom can more easily be achieved without the need to build upwards. In light airs, a trimaran can be 'balanced' on its centre hull, thus reducing wetted surface area. The motion is 'softer' — more similar to a keelboat's, but of course heeling nothing like as much. An auxiliary engine is more easily installed within the central hull (although larger catamarans can have an engine in both hulls, greatly improving their manoeuvrability under power).

But perhaps the trimaran's most important advantage is that, with regard to capsize, it tends to be more forgiving and gives clearer warnings that the risk exists. Whereas a catamaran may be sailing splendidly right up to the point where it flips, a trimaran will start to labour and give other indications of distress. I can tell you hand on heart that to see the lee hull dive beneath the waves can have you shortening sail faster than any other stimulus I know.

The arguments in favour of the trimaran diminish as size increases. Whereas a smallish trimaran — of say 30 ft (9.14m) LOA — would undoubtedly be safer offshore than an equivalent catamaran (for the reasons stated in the previous paragraph), any differences become increasingly academic in larger, more stable boats. This is because, as we have already discussed, form stability (on which all multihulls solely rely) is increasing with size by the power of four. Very large catamarans are so inherently stable anyway that any marginal advantage the tri might offer would pale besides the awkwardness of its horrendous beam.

A custom built trimaran, designed by the author, beached in Galveston Bay. The convenience of very shallow draught is clearly apparent.

Chapter 10

THE ACCOMMODATION

As launching parties go it was a sumptuous affair. The new 71 ft (21.64m) schooner lay snugly in her berth, the christening champagne already drying on her bow. The owner — a merchant banker, I seem to recall — was accepting the congratulations of his guests in gracious manner, steering them towards the trays of canapes and drinks laid out in the enormous saloon.

Down below, the decor was breathtaking. Apparently the owner's wife — French and *trés chic* — had a hand in its design. A deep carpet lay underfoot. The colour scheme was in soft greys and pinks with slate working surfaces trimmed with brushed stainless steel. There was not a piece of wood in sight. A visual symphony in modernism, I was told. A paean in praise of polymerisation.

I was newly into yacht design then, still poor and the owner of a small plywood bilge keeler, the coffin-like interior of which had just enough room to contain only the most rudimentary amenities. Now, wandering around on that immense ship, I felt like the designer of small bungalows being confronted by the Taj Mahal. Impressed almost to reverence, I sought the company of an old friend, a crusty old yachting journalist of blistering wit.

'Terrific, isn't it?' I gushed, indicating this vast open space with a sweep of my arm. Even with the hundred-or-so people aboard, it barely seemed crowded.

'Think so?' my friend responded, stuffing down another *vol-au-vent* and peering at me over his half glasses. 'Like it, eh?'

I nodded enthusiastically. 'Of course! Who wouldn't? Look at all that space. My front room at home's smaller than this!'

The *vol-au-vent* was followed by a large swig of wine. He took time to wipe his mouth with the back of his hand. 'Yes, but your front room at home doesn't heel to thirty degrees. Imagine this bloody thing at sea. You'd need a couple of Sherpas to help you to the weather side!'

And, of course, he was right. A few years later I saw the same boat in the Caribbean. It had changed hands by then. A small forest of pillars had sprung up in that wondrous open saloon, providing the handholds it had previously lacked. Naturally, this somewhat detracted from the visual impact as originally conceived, but at least the yacht now looked tenable.

For boats, like spaceships, must be designed to be workable at crazy angles. As we've said before, what may be attractive alongside can become positively hellish when tossed about a bit. Sometimes, in their eagerness to provide as many of the 'comforts of home' as possible, designers go overboard on the interior appointments, and a stiff price is paid in terms of practicality. Comfort is obviously important to all of us but it has to be tempered with common sense. The best kind of yacht combines *reasonable* living space in port with convenience and safety at sea. As with many other aspects of design, this involves an interlocking set of considerations, every one of which affects the others.

Of course the problem is more acute in smaller boats. Very large yachts, by virtue of their internal volume, can be generous with the accommodation, and this allows the designer more flexibility in choice. On the other hand, small to medium sized boats exert tighter dimensional limitations on what can be done, and this has to be accepted. The twenty-footer simply cannot provide the same accommodation as a thirty-footer; and neither can the thirty-footer that of a forty-footer, and so on. To attempt the impossible invariably ruins the boat.

So, let's now ignore the giant yachts (and, for the moment, multihulls), and limit ourselves to boats in the sort of bracket ordinary mortals can expect to own. Basically, a sailboat must provide somewhere from which to steer (the **cockpit**), somewhere to live (the **cabin**), somewhere to sleep (the **berths**), somewhere to navigate (the **chart table**), somewhere to cook (the **galley**), and somewhere to go to toilet (the **heads**).

The main issues affecting interior design are:

Crew size. As we mentioned earlier, this is usually less than one would suppose and it pays to be realistic. Four berths are usually enough on a 30 ft (9.14m) yacht, and six on one of 40 ft (12.19m). Space taken up providing unwanted berths can often be put to better use.

Climate. This determines whether life aboard is to be conducted mainly on deck or below. Northern European boats tend to have small, sheltered cockpits and large cabins where one can cower from the weather. Boats from hotter areas are more likely to have larger cockpits (perhaps with an awning or 'bimini' over to keep off the sun), and smaller cabins, just sufficient to cook and sleep in. Our own boat, *Spook,*

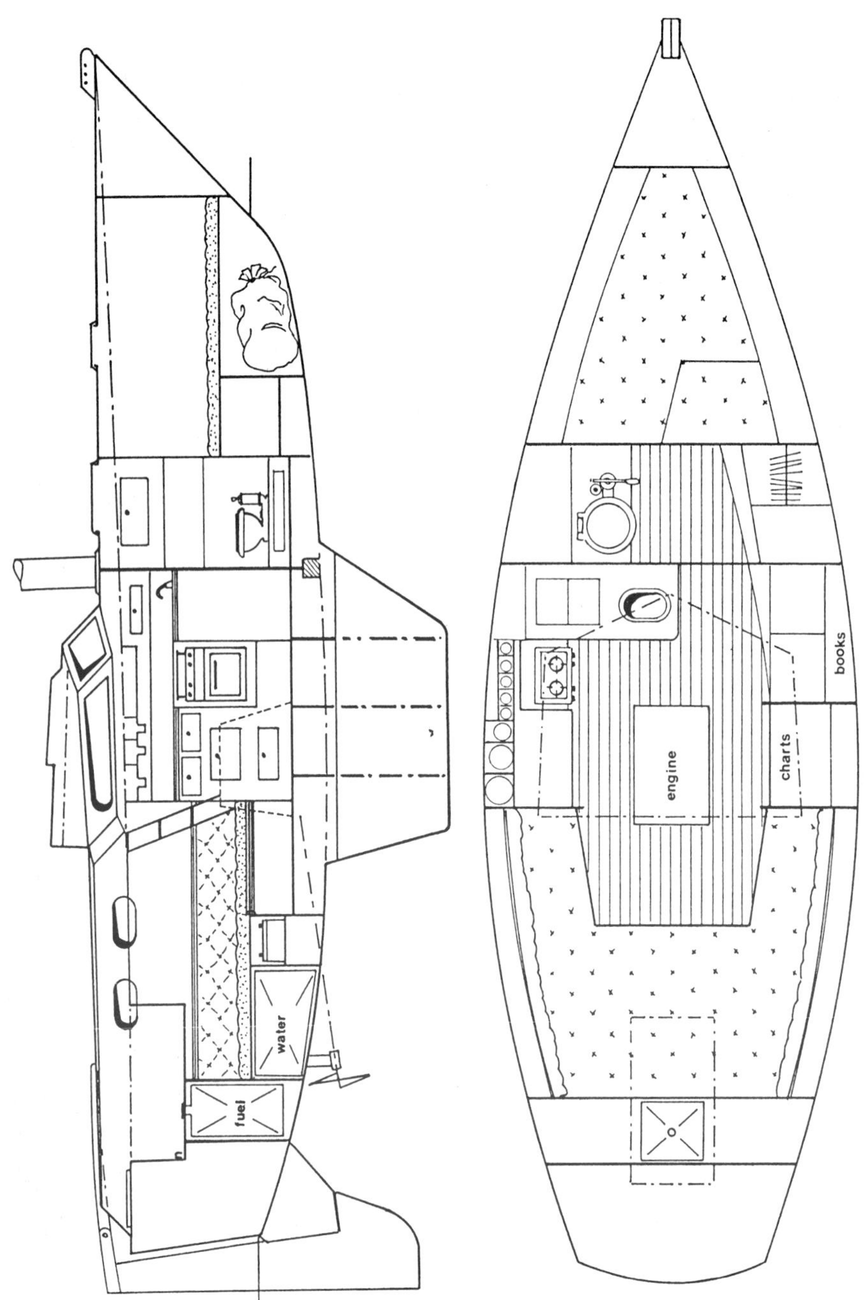
fuel
water
engine
charts
books

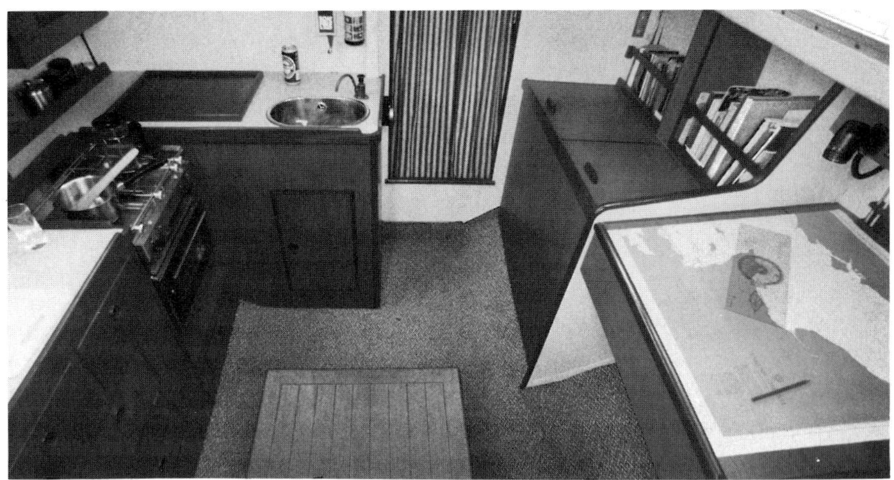

Spook's *working area. The view down the companionway. The navigation space is to starboard, the galley to port. The engine box forms a convenient seat.*

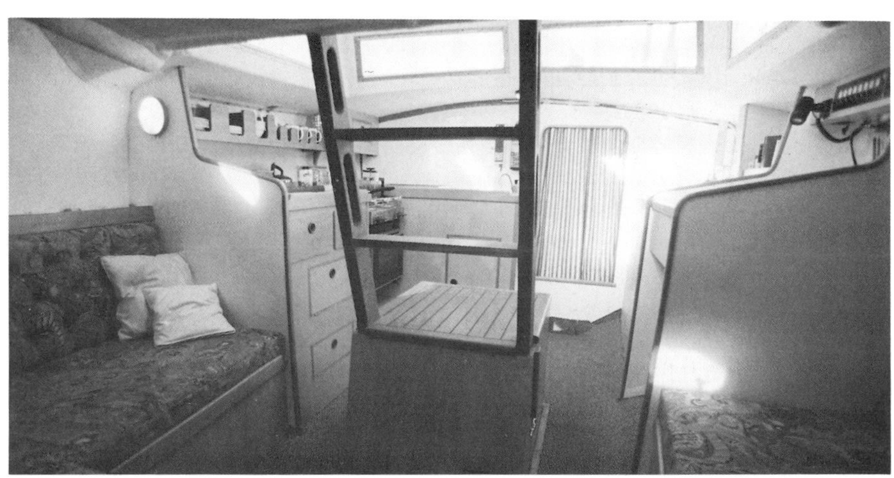

Spook's *interior, looking forward from the full width seating area.*

was designed for the Mediterranean and, with her open cockpit and large deck area, is very much in the latter tradition.

Type of cruising intended. This obviously relates to considerations of both climate and crew size. A family of four thinking of week-ending along the coast is bound to have very different requirements than the young couple planning a two year circumnavigation. The coastal cruiser may be quite satisfied to settle for a small galley and a makeshift chart table in favour of better seating, whereas the reverse would be the case for the circumnavigator.

Privacy. Obviously a personal issue. Even some family groups prefer a compartmentalized interior lay-out so that they can closet themselves into their own separate cabins when they want to. Others will prefer the open-plan approach, trading some loss of privacy for feelings of spaciousness. In *Spook* we've elected to follow this last principle — sailing only with the kind of people who would be comfortable in that open, unconcealed environment.

Spook's lay-out is worth examining. As can be seen in Figure 6, it's rather unusual. All of the working functions are clustered around the foot of the companionway. Standing in this position, whether at the galley or chart table, it's possible to maintain an all-round watch through the dog-house windows. The seating area, under the cockpit bridge-deck, provides a double berth athwartship for use in port, and two singles with **lee cloths** (canvas sides which can be rigged to stop you rolling out) for use in heavy weather at sea. Forward, there is the toilet compartment and a double berth for occasional guests.

Spook is unquestionably a two person boat, with enough accommodation to entertain another couple for short periods. For us, her lay-out works very well indeed, being both comfortable and convenient. Within the limitations of her 30' 6" (9.30m) size, she is all we could ask for. Of course, as we designed and built her to meet our own specific needs, it would be surprising if we were now disappointed. But, although there must be hundreds of other couples with similar requirements as ourselves, you would be very unlikely to find such an accommodation plan offered by a production builder. Pursuing the dictum that 'berths sell' *Spook* simply doesn't offer enough of that commodity.

But, in pursuit of marketability, I believe it's possible to spoil an otherwise sensible boat by dividing its interior into too many small boxes. Recently, I was proudly shown over a new 33 ft (10.06m) sloop. With its centre cockpit lay-out, it boasted seven berths in three separate cabins and, as if that wasn't enough, it also had two enclosed toilet compartments, one of which contained a shower. The physical price paid for this prodigious ingenuity of design was an overall feeling of claustrophobia and an almost total lack of stowage space on deck. Nearly every cubic inch had been utilised to store people. Room for such deck gear as the inflatable dinghy, the bags of sails, the fenders, and all the other bits of pieces that are part of a yacht's essential equipment had been forgotten in the quest for maximised accommodation. Not surprisingly, the owner was now nonplussed trying to decide where to stow everything.

Of course there are sometimes very sound reasons for wanting to split the accommodation — shared ownership being the most common — in which case the centre cockpit yacht does offer a convenient way of achieving this. However, unless the boat is of fair size — say, more than 35 ft (10.67m) LOA — then the inevitable consequence will be tiny, cramped cabins which, although undoubtedly private, are not likely to be very comfortable.

But accommodation isn't just about places to sit and sleep. Important amenities must be provided. Of these, perhaps the most vital is the galley.

Galleys can range from the basic to lavish. In 1970 my Round Britain Race trimaran entry *Three Fingered Jack* was boarded by the official race scrutineers, H.G. 'Blondie' Hasler (Cockleshell Hero and co-instigator with Francis Chichester of the Singlehanded Transatlantic Race) and Bernard Hayman (then editor of Yachting World). After examining all the safety gear they came to my 'galley' — a primitive, single-burner, gas cartridge picnic stove screwed to a shelf. After over twenty years, my memory is too hazy to recount the ensuing conversation verbatim but I recall that Bernard Hayman viewed it with some distaste and, indeed, actually questioned whether it qualified as a galley within the meaning of the race rules. Blondie Hasler, on the other hand, was far more enthusiastic and took to muttering about having cooked three course dinners on less.

At that time I inclined towards Hasler's simplistic philosophy, but as the years pass by I find myself increasingly subscribing to the view as expressed by Hayman. Good food is vital to enjoyable cruising and, although it can be created on a handful of smouldering sticks, it's obviously more convenient to have decent equipment aboard. *Spook* has a **gimbaled** (suspended so that it stays level regardless of the angle of the boat) butane fuelled two-burner hob with an integral grill and oven. An electric top-loading refrigerator chills the wine and keeps the salad fresh, and a stainless steel sink is at hand for the washing-up. On these Chele works miracles and we eat at sea probably better than we do at home.

Choice of fuel for the cooker can be important. The most convenient by far is liquefied petroleum gas (either butane or propane — generally known as LPG) carried in rechargeable cylinders. It produces a very hot flame and is entirely clean. However, not all systems are interchangeable, and you need to ensure that the type of cylinders you carry can be exchanged in the areas you wish to cruise. The down side for LPG is that, without doubt, this is the most dangerous type of fuel. As both butane and propane are heavier than air, any leakage could drain into the bilge where, when mixed with air to a certain concentration, it can explode if accidentally ignited. Gas cylinders should be stowed in vented lockers and the entire installation must be meticulously installed and maintained. But, despite the risks, the sheer convenience of LPG gas attracts many yachtsmen, and there are tens of thousands of such installations in use around the world.

Perhaps the next most favoured fuel is paraffin or kerosene. Surprisingly, this isn't as freely available as one might suppose — I once had a terrible job obtaining some in Spain — but usually enough can be carried aboard to last for months or even years. Paraffin cooks about as quickly as LPG but is rather smelly.

Alcohol (methylated spirits) fuelled cookers are popular in some areas — notably Scandinavia and the United States. These are the safest available but the flame is relatively cool and, as a consequence, cooks very slowly. Of all the fuels, alcohol is the most expensive to buy and the most difficult to obtain in some parts of the world (somewhat disconcertingly, we once bought a couple of gallons from a rum distillery in the West Indies!). Although obviously a matter of opinion, I also thinks it smells revolting.

Although gas burning refrigerators were once common, these proved unreliable (and potentially dangerous), and are no longer generally available. Today's yacht refrigerator will either be driven directly from the engine (using a modified automobile air-conditioning compressor) or powered electrically from the boat's supply. Electric refrigerators fall into two distinct types: The most powerful use a Freon charged compressor to cool down an evaporator or eutectic plate. The second type uses a solid state unit (with a small fan being the only moving part) based on a principle known as the Peltier Effect. These are rather less efficient in terms of both cooling ability and current drain but are very compact and much quieter than compressor units.

Lavatorial conversation isn't the stuff of most cocktail parties, but the subject figures large and loud in many yacht club bars. Sailors are slaves to their toilets. The days when bucket-and-chuck-it would suffice for all but the most wimpish have long gone. In the modern sailboat the **heads** (from an area in the bows of old sailing ships where seats were suspended over open water for the use of early mariners) is a vital, and often devilish, part of the boat's inventory, about which (Sigmund, don't bother to note) sailors have an unhealthy preoccupation.

A marine toilet pumps effluent either directly into the sea or into a holding tank where it can be discharged later into proper disposal facilities. The use of holding tanks is especially common in areas which have no (or perhaps only a sluggish) tidal flow. This includes most inland waterways, the United States, and various other coastal areas. Sometimes these rules are waived for visiting yachts passing through, but not always. If travelling abroad, check in advance. To even unwittingly break mandatory pollution control laws could attract severe penalties.

I must confess to being a card carrying member of the *I Loathe Loos Society*. Their usefulness is indisputable, but their predisposition to malfunction without any apparent provocation has been known to tip sane men over the edge. Now, I know that being a marine toilet isn't a lot of fun, but sometimes their antics seem almost malevolent, as if they were getting their own back for what we do to them. Marine toilets require treating deferentially, like operatic divas on the brink of nervous breakdowns. Abuse them in any way and they have a capacity for revenge which you will rue to witness. The one aboard Spook is made up from the pieces of three toilets previously thrown out by infuriated owners. Actually, in truth it now works rather well. Divide and conquer, perhaps?

Fancier yachts often have showers built into the heads compartment. Usually this involves drawing a curtain about yourself whilst the shower sprinkles water over your body in the accepted fashion. On the face of it this would seem like a great idea but sometimes the designers haven't quite thought the matter through. Sailing with a friend on his nice new boat, I once expressed a wish to take a shower — *the* shower he had been bragging about since he had ordered the boat some months previously. But, instead of the expected nod to 'feel free' or 'help yourself', consternation gripped him and he started to mumble about conserving water and 'maybe the marina tomorrow would be a better bet'. Eventually he confessed that showering hadn't turned out to be the pleasure he had anticipated. Casting off your clothes and plunging into the deluge was apparently only the finale to a fairly lengthy preamble. First you had to virtually empty the heads of all its contents: toilet paper from the holder, dry towels from the locker, medicines from the first aid cabinet — everything that could be damaged by the swirl of droplets and steam that filled that tiny cubicle. Then, of course, after the event there was the mopping up to do, and the pumping out of the soapy water that was sloshing around somewhere in the bilge. As he sadly remarked: 'Boats get quite wet enough without inviting the bloody stuff in. I'm afraid I've reverted to a bucket on the foredeck.'

Of particular interest to me is the navigation space, about which I have strong opinions. Perhaps I've been spoiled by the spacious chartrooms of the merchant ships on which I served, but I find the sums and chartwork so much easier to do in well fashioned surroundings. Most boats of reasonable size provide a chart table, but not all are as suitable or as practical as they might seem at first sight. The commonly seen sit-down navigator's area, where the head of a berth provides the seat, might be fine during the day in good weather, but what about at night when it's raining and (a) your oilskins are sopping wet and you don't want to soak the upholstery, or (b) the head of a sleeping crew member rests on the very spot where you'd like to plant your stern? Personally, I prefer to stand up at the chart table in a position not far from the companionway, where it doesn't matter who's sleeping where or how wet I am. Unfortunately, this arrangement is unusual on production boats.

Chart tables should be of adequate size — at least large enough to take a chart folded just once — and robust enough to be leaned against heavily. The space around it should provide for the stowage of all the books and charts you will need, plus the electronic instrumentation that's so much a part of navigation today. The poky little navigation space, built in more as a token fixture than a proper work station, is just about useless. In these cases the saloon table would probably suffice better, the wasted space being put to better use.

Multihulls can either provide a fantastic amount of accommodation or very little. The average cruising multi with its high volume form is immensely commodious for any given length. On the other hand, sailing a racing flyer with its needle-like hulls is rather like living in a drain pipe.

Trimarans, except the very largest, are a little like monohulls in configuration. The accommodation is usually limited to the centre hull, with berth and locker space spilling over into the 'wings'. Because the centre hull has a narrow waterline beam, **sole** (floor) space is often limited. Larger trimarans also have accommodation in the amas and are very spacious indeed.

The modern cruising catamaran, with its central bridge-deck saloon and two hulls, offers a wide choice of lay-out. Typically, the central area, with its limited headroom, is used for seating and dining, and the hulls for cooking and sleeping. Because of the naturally compartmentalized shape of the catamaran, a good deal of privacy is achievable.

A feature of all multihulls is that they sail almost upright. Consequently, regardless of the point of sail, all of the accommodation remains tenable when at sea. Cookers can be non-gimballed, lee cloths are unnecessary, and it's possible to sleep on the inward or leeward side as you wish. This contrasts markedly with the average monohull, in which it's often difficult to remain in the windward bunks with the yacht hard pressed.

Chapter 11

THE CONSTRUCTION

Let's take time to consider the way in which boats are built. Concept and design are all very well but, at the end of the day, someone must hew a log, weld a metal plate, or make himself sticky with resin in order that a boat can be physically realised.

Boatbuilding is an ancient craft whose principles of development are still largely extant. Primitive dug-out canoes still do daily service in many parts of the world. Reed boats continue to carry fishermen in Mexico and the Middle East. And even in the western world, where sophisticated techniques now dominate, a few specialised craftsmen still painstakingly build in the traditional manner, happily over-subscribed by customers clamouring for their work.

Today's sailors are the beneficiaries of this long and continuous heritage. For them the choice is wide.

Glass Reinforced Plastics: Often called 'fibreglass', **GRP**, or **FRP** (in the USA) for short. GRP boats make up by far the majority of those sold over the past twenty years.

So, what exactly is GRP? In one important respect it is unique, for it is a material of construction which is actually made in situ and, therefore, there is virtually no limit to the size of objects that can be 'seamlessly' fabricated. Basically it is a composite of a durable resin (usually polyester) reinforced with an immensely strong fibrous glass. The resin is activated with a catalyst and applied in liquid form to the reinforcement. Within minutes it sets hard, binding the reinforcement into a robust and almost impervious material.

The history of man-made plastic materials goes back to 1862 when an Englishman, Alexander Parkes, produced a substance which he called *Parkesine* — a forerunner of Celluloid. Plastics are made by a process known as *polymerisation* where long chain molecules are formed — each with differing physical properties. Polyester is one such polymer.

Although other reinforcements (such as carbon and aramid fibres) are increasingly used, glass fibre is the one that concerns us most at present. It is made by rapidly drawing and cooling molten glass and, although the technique has been known since the Egyptian 18th Dynasty (about 1500 B.C.), it was not until the 1930's that suitable fibres became commercially available.

Boatbuilders tend to be a conservative bunch but they took to GRP with alacrity. By the early sixties wooden boats were being nudged aside by the wonder material. And by the seventies GRP had become so well established that there was hardly anything else available. Speed of construction was that major attraction — quite marvellous in comparison with other more laborious methods. Mass production had come to boatbuilding, and prices tumbled. Freed of the constraints of timber and steel, designers were revelling in the complexity of the shapes they could now draw. The publicity men were delirious with excitement. 'Maintenance free!' 'Lifetime guaranteed!' Some even claimed that the surfaces were so smooth that barnacles couldn't cling to them.

And they were partially right, though not about the barnacles, which will cling as tenaciously to fibreglass as any other surface. GRP laminates are incredibly durable. They don't rot and they don't rust. They are self-coloured and only require painting after many seasons use. You can hardly blame the early publicists for believing that the everlasting boat was at hand.

But then along came osmosis.

For nature has a way of deflating exalted claims, and thus it proved with GRP. If viewed microscopically, the smooth plastic finish could be seen to be a honeycomb of little voids and crevices. Over the years boats were becoming heavier and (horror of horrors!) it suddenly dawned on someone that the unthinkable was happening — they were absorbing water! Some even developed rashes of fluid-filled blisters on their underwater surfaces — 'boat pox' or, somewhat misleadingly, 'osmosis' had arrived to chasten the smug. There is no other word which can strike such terror into the heart of a GRP yacht owner. I've seen grown men quake, their knees buckling at the news of their boat's pimply affliction.

Water absorption in its various forms is the Achilles heel of the GRP boat. It happens very slowly but it is a reality which must be faced. Modern resins are very much better than those of twenty years ago. Technology has moved on. But, although these developments have done a lot to help, even the most modern boats will still soak up water to some extent. The word 'osmosis' actually describes just one of the specific mechanisms of absorption, but has been adopted as a generic term to cover the whole topic, especially where visible blistering is found.

But there has been widespread over-reaction. These problems *do* exist but they are usually treatable and, to a large extent, can be minimised or even prevented with specialised coatings. Twenty-year-old boats are

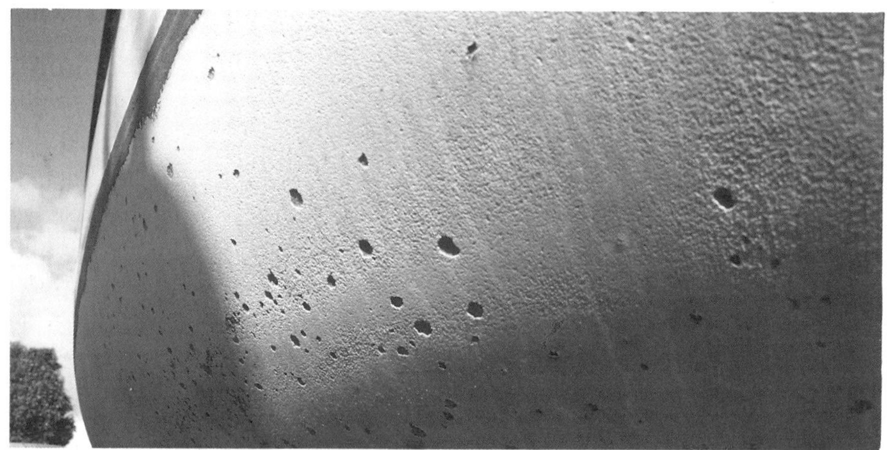

Osmosis — the scourge of GRP. The blisters here have been opened up by grit blasting.

commonplace, and there's no reason why many of those shouldn't go on to serve another twenty, and perhaps twenty beyond that. A very high proportion of all the fibreglass boats ever built are still in service — a considerable headache for the boatbuilding industry, who would prefer them to disappear. GRP is a superb engineering material which brings a huge selection of boats within the financial reach of thousands. It is deservedly popular and will undoubtedly remain so.

Most GRP boats are laminated from the outside in, using large 'female' moulds (also usually made of GRP). The inside face of the mould must be highly polished, for this will determine the *external* finish of the completed hull. Waxes are used to improve this finish and also to act as a 'release agent' to prevent the resins sticking to the mould surface.

Construction starts with a pigmented resin **gelcoat** being applied to the inside of the mould. This will eventually form the coloured exterior coating of the hull. Then the GRP skin is 'laid up' in successive layers to the required thickness, adding extra material in highly stressed areas. After a few days the laminate will have hardened and fully 'cured' (achieved full strength), and the hull can be released from the mould and transferred to another part of the factory for completion.

Deck mouldings and, sometimes, parts of the internal structure are laminated in similar fashion and the whole assembly is bonded together rather like a colossal plastic model kit. Usually, for convenience of access, the interior fitments and such items as the engine are installed before the deck is fitted to the hull. Although there may be some variation in procedure details, nearly all production boatbuilders construct their products in this way.

Techniques also exist for producing GRP one-offs — such as my own yacht *Spook* — but descriptions of these methods are necessarily detailed and rather beyond the scope of this book. Custom building is obviously more expensive but it does give you *exactly* the boat you want. Even doing-it-yourself is feasible. If you are willing to take the trouble, GRP construction need not be limited to what the production builders are prepared to offer.

Wood — Traditional construction: From the time in prehistory when man first sat astride a log to carry him over the water, wood has been used in the construction of boats. Presumably, it later occurred to him that if he hollowed out his log he could actually sit inside it and stay dry. Later still, as his ambitions grew, he realised that single logs were just not big enough for the vessels he now wanted. So, he developed methods of shaping and joining a number of logs together, and thus became the first shipwright.

A small clinker built centre-boarder.

Boats are still built like this today. Although power tools have greatly reduced the labour involved, many of the techniques remain basically the same. The traditionally constructed vessel is still a complicated structure comprised of hundreds of wooden components, each individually shaped and assembled with the kind of fastenings and joints known to shipwrights for centuries.

Two distinct types are common: **Carvel** construction, where the planking is laid edge to edge, presenting a flush exterior surface; and **clinker** or **lapstrake** where the planks are allowed to overlap each other and the exterior surface appears 'stepped'. The latter is usually found only in smaller craft.

The way a traditionally built boat creaks and groans when sailing can be alarming to those more accustomed to integrated constructional methods such as GRP or steel. Some 'move' so much when hard pressed that they perceptibly twist out of shape. A favourite trick on one boat I sailed was to change tack when someone was in the heads, whereupon the door would jam solid; and it would require another alteration of course to release the victim. Hardly surprisingly, this movement means that few traditional boats are entirely watertight. Most leak to some extent and require regular pumping out.

The greatest scourge of timber is fungal attack — either **wet rot** or **dry rot,** the former being by far the most common and the latter the most serious. Wet rot tends to remain localised whilst dry rot spreads rapidly. On some timber boats I have seen, the condition was found to be so extensive that the phrase 'rotten as a carrot' seemed rather harsh on the carrot. Rot-causing fungi develop in areas which are damp, warm, and poorly ventilated — which often means in dark corners hidden from view. Sea water is quite an effective fungicide so, contrary to common belief, the exteriors of hulls rarely rot.

Different timbers have varying degrees of resistance to rot. For example: teak and iroko are very durable; mahogany and oak are moderately durable; and spruce and ash are considered non-durable. It therefore follows that the choice of timber has a crucial bearing on the longevity of any traditional yacht.

Marine borers pose another serious threat. In European waters a small woodlouse-like creature called *gribble* likes to lunch on unprotected planking. In the tropics the shipworm *teredo* actually goes searching for wood to eat. As with rot, some timbers are more resistant than others. Early hulls were first protected against marine borers with copious applications of pitch. Later, thin copper sheathing was used,

The ravages of rot: affected planking cut away for replacement.

which not only deterred the borers but, due to its mild toxicity, also inhibited the growth of barnacles and marine vegetation.

Traditional boats can be almost interminably repaired. As they are an assemblage of separate pieces, these pieces can be replaced individually if they deteriorate. Nelson's flagship *HMS Victory*, now displayed in dry dock in Portsmouth, has been so extensively rebuilt over the years that there must be very little of the original ship left.

But it has to be accepted that traditional timber vessels require more maintenance than other forms of construction. Although there is no reason why such boats shouldn't be every bit as seaworthy as their more modern counterparts, it will require rather more effort to keep them that way.

Wood — Modern techniques: The development of new waterproof adhesives heralded a resurgence of interest in timber construction.

Marine plywoods emerged about 1950 and, as previously discussed, were greeted eagerly by the designers and boatbuilders of the day. But plywood panels can only be bent in one axis at a time and, although ideal for flattish areas such as decks and cabin sides, this limitation made hull shapes somewhat crude.

During the Second World War certain aircraft — most notably the DeHavilland *Mosquito* — were built using laminates of thin veneers to form monocoque compound shapes. This technology, too, was both adopted and adapted and, around the mid-fifties, another aircraft builder — now trading as Fairey Marine — had turned to boatbuilding and was producing the remarkable 26 ft *Atalanta* by a hot moulding method using vacuum bags and heated autoclaves. The *Atalanta* has a pronouncedly curved shape, both for the hull and deck, and is immensely strong and durable, despite her light displacement of only 2 tons. Many remain afloat today, none the worse for their years. From the engineering standpoint, a wooden boat hull could at last be regarded as one-piece, with all that meant in terms of structural integrity and watertightness.

The next important milestone was the arrival of epoxy resin glues, capable of forming bonds more powerful than the wood itself. In Michigan, U.S.A., the Gougeon brothers, Meade, Jan, and Joe, were putting the final touches to what they were to call their WEST system — the word WEST being a rather misleading acronym for *Wet Epoxy Saturation Technique* (no glue can actually *saturate* timber — it will only penetrate a little way into the surface). The WEST system involves reducing the moisture content of the wood (it also becomes stronger when dry) to the point where it would more readily soak up the epoxy used both to bond and coat it.

Timber is a first rate structural material which, when worked with suitable adhesives, can now be integrated into forms which can almost be considered homogeneous. With the surfaces well protected and every minute crevice filled with resin, the chances of rot have been greatly reduced. Sheathing externally with a light glass cloth and epoxy resin — the modern equivalent of copper cladding — will keep the gribble and teredo at bay. Although yet to be fully tested by time itself, it's my bet that the modern wooden yacht will show itself to be extremely long-lived — probably outlasting the equivalent GRP boat.

Obviously such a method is very labour intensive and professional building costs are high. However, many amateur builders have been attracted to epoxy/timber construction and there is a wide selection of plans to choose from, both monohull and multihull.

Steel: Welded steel construction is a firm favourite amongst long-distance sailors. It is tremendously strong and very forgiving. I recently saw a boat in Mallorca which had been blown ashore onto a rocky promontory. Almost all of the starboard side had been stove in by the pounding. But, although the hull skin had been dented inwards at least a foot in some places, it remained unpunctured. The yacht was eventually floated off and towed to safety. I doubt if any other form of construction would have survived such a terrible battering.

And, say the long-distance sailors, that's not the end of the story. The beauty of steel, they will tell you, is that you can get it repaired almost anywhere. Minor damage can usually just be hammered out. Anything more serious can be cut away and a new piece welded in. Even in the remotest places, you will find a source of steel and someone with the necessary equipment to work it.

But we live in an imperfect world, and everything has its down side. Steel boats require insulation, both thermal and acoustic. Although not as bad as is sometimes alleged, they can be hot in the tropics and noisy in heavy conditions — 'living in a boiler with the riveters still working on the outside' was one overstated description I heard. Cosmetically, they can also be rather unpleasing. No matter how skilfully it might be worked, steel plating buckles when welded. Many steel boats have the appearance of well kicked cans and, in order to improve this, the fancier boatyards screed their topsides with cement to fill in the inevitable hollows. Obviously this adds weight — a significant amount on a small boat if the hull was very unfair — and the filler can fall out in the event of even a fairly minor collision or bump when coming alongside. To see your topsides turn deciduous can be disconcerting. Personally, I would prefer to accept the *honest* unfairness in the plating, rather than to have it concealed behind an unknown thickness of cement.

And steel boats also have their maintenance problems. Rust is the principal enemy and, in this regard, it's hard to imagine a more demanding environment than a salty sea. The situation is somewhat analogous to rot in a timber vessel — the interior is most at risk. Any little pockets of standing water will cause corrosion and designers do their utmost to 'design them out'. Owners wage constant war against rust — the most frequently used weapon being a paint brush.

Although steel is often used for building smaller yachts — particularly in Holland where it is something of a tradition — it becomes very much more successful as size increases. Because of the obvious weight penalties, the smaller the yacht the thinner must be the steel. Thin plating is more prone to buckling when welded, and even relatively minor areas of corrosion can rapidly eat their way right through to form pinhole leaks.

Sky, *an impressive ocean cruising cutter, built in steel by her owner Roger Waskett, in a rural English garden.*

Aluminium: Only a third the weight of steel, rust-proof and less acoustically resonant — it would seem the perfect material with which to build boats. Tremendous advances have been made in developing alloys for use in marine environments, and the specialised techniques needed to weld them. So why aren't there more aluminium yachts?

The main reason is expense. Not only is the aluminium itself more costly than steel, but it is also more difficult to handle. Most marine alloys are of a 'work hardening' type — that is to say they become harder and more brittle when bent or formed — and cannot be hammered around with quite the abandon of mild steel. Also, welding is more critical, requiring meticulous working methods and more elaborate and costly equipment.

Virtually nothing sticks well to aluminium, making painting a problem. The French, ever the pragmatists, often don't bother, and one frequently sees dull grey yachts flying their national tricolour.

And, although aluminium is very corrosion resistant in its own right, combine it with certain other metals and that situation can change disastrously. For aluminium lives towards the least noble end of the galvanic series. This means that when submerged in sea water (which acts as an electrolyte) in conjunction with a more noble metal, it will behave like the anodic side of a battery cell and will be galvanically eroded. In practical terms this rules out such boatbuilding standards as bronze skin fittings and seacocks. Even less obvious threats such as paints containing copper, lead, or mercury can also cause irreparable damage.

Designers and builders must always keep a weather eye open for such combinations, but even then things can go badly wrong. I was once involved in a case where the owner of an expensive aluminium yacht was horrified to see holes suddenly appearing in his hull. Upon investigation it turned out that he had recently hired an automobile electrician to install a new stereo system in the cabin. This electrician, drawing innocently upon his normal work experience, had used the hull itself to provide one side of the supply circuit, thus immediately undoing all the care that had gone before to make the aluminium structure electrically inactive.

Notwithstanding the horror stories, aluminium is still worth considering if you can afford it. If properly designed and scrupulously put together, the very real advantages of the aluminium yacht can be safely enjoyed.

Ferro-cement: I can recall my own astonishment when I first heard about concrete boats. The idea seemed so preposterous and I can distinctly remember wondering if I'd been the victim of some kind of joke. Talk of bridges and buildings and other such massive and monolithic structures, and I had no difficulty imagining an appropriate role for concrete. But the delicate forms of a sailboat? Hardly.

Well, luckily someone else had already been more imaginative than myself — and a century and a half earlier, too. In 1824 it occurred to the Frenchman Joseph Louis Lambot that concrete and iron made a happy combination. Structurally, concrete was excellent in compression, but poor in tension. Iron, on the other hand, performed splendidly in tension and — as if to confirm that here was an engineering marriage made in heaven — had an almost identical coefficient of expansion, and would therefore shrink and expand in response to any temperature changes in perfect harmony with the concrete. Lambot went on to build two small boats which survive to this day.

Since then ferro-cement has been used to build vessels of widely diverse types. Small ships, fishing boats, ferries, and yachts — even the *Mulberry* harbours of the Normandy invasion. Although construction is very labour-intensive, the cost of the basic materials is extremely low and offers attractive commercial advantages, particularly to under-developed countries. The Chinese, for example, have an established tradition of ferro-cement boatbuilding, supplying a range of smaller work boats at a fraction of the cost of wood or steel. And these same financial benefits attract amateur boatbuilders who, with nothing more than a few simple tools, have built some amazingly large yachts.

It's important not to think of ferro-cement in quite the same light as the concrete slab on which your house sits. Whereas the latter was poured as a sloppy mixture containing only a comparatively small proportion of cement, ferro-cement boatbuilding requires a very rich mortar (usually 1 part cement to 2 parts sand) of a nearly dry consistency, which is applied by carefully 'plastering' over a densely constructed steel reinforcement. It is this plastering which is the most critical part of the whole process. The entire hull must be completed in one continuous operation, and often involves large teams of men. But, if done properly, the resulting composite is extremely strong and surprisingly flexible — in many ways similar to wood.

As with other materials, ferro-cement has its snags. The main one is the impracticability of constructing thin-skinned hulls, and the consequent weight penalty of this limitation. Typically the minimum attainable thickness is 5/8" (15 mm) which, compared to mahogany, would in weight terms be equivalent to planking nearly 3" thick (though this is a somewhat misleading comparison because it disregards the additional weight of all the framing required on a wooden boat). For this reason it is rare to see ferro-cement boats of less than 35 feet and even these tend to be of above average displacement.

But perhaps the main disadvantage is not technical at all, but one of general perception. Although there are some superb ferro-cement yachts around, there are also many which are downright awful — often the grisly creations of home builders having more enthusiasm than ability. Ferro-cement has had a bad press over the years, and the folk who run the banks and the insurance companies have taken note. Although it's undoubtedly unfair to the type as a whole, a ferro-cement boat is often difficult to insure, difficult to finance and, when you've done with it, difficult to *sell*.

So, where does this all leave us? As you can see, all forms of construction have their good and bad points. There is no 'perfect' material; if there was we would all be using it. Personal preference, cash limitations, willingness to toil or pay for upkeep, suitability for the purpose in mind — all hold sway in the choice we must make.

But it is possible to make some generalisations. For most cruising yachtsmen, the ease of maintenance and the widest selection of designs available leads us almost inevitably towards GRP. The long distance or live-aboard sailor can attend to his boat almost on a daily basis, so steel or wood could be practical. Aluminium alloy or the more exotic forms of timber construction would be a good choice for the performance minded, because both lend themselves ideally to very light displacement. And the heavy ferro-cement boat, unlovely and unromantic though the material might be, often provides more boat for your money than any other type around.

CLASSIFICATION:

Before we leave the subject of construction, it's worth saying something about classification societies. These organisations exist to lay down constructional specifications for ship and boat builders, and to monitor the way they are built. A vessel constructed to the rules of such a classification, and issued with a certificate affirming this, will be known to be of a quality at least to that determined standard.

The most stringent of these classifications (such as Lloyd's 100 A1) involves compliance with very rigid rules regarding choice of materials, **scantling** (sizes of components), installation methods for all fittings and machinery, and quality of workmanship. The vessel will be inspected periodically during construction and, once completed, will continue to be surveyed at regular intervals during its life to confirm that the vessel is maintained to that standard and, therefore, stays 'in class'.

Other, less demanding classifications, may require the production boatbuilder to submit plans for approval and, thereafter, to allow occasional inspection of his work to ensure specified standards are being adhered to. Some only relate to the hull structure.

The oldest and most famous classification society is Lloyd's Register of Shipping, named after a Mr Edward Lloyd who, in the 17th Century, owned the coffee shop in the City of London in which the idea was originally hatched.

Other societies include the American Bureau of Shipping, Bureau Veritas, Det Norske Veritas, and Germanischer Lloyd — all of whom perform more or less the same functions.

Although classifications are meaningful and can tell you something about the quality of the boat, they can also be misleading and open to abuse. Particularly be wary of expressions such as 'Built in excess of Lloyd's' or 'Hull to Lloyd's specification'. These may simply mean that the builder has dipped casually into his copy of the specifications (assuming he has one, which he may well not), and adopted *part* of them without regard to the whole. For instance, he could have moulded his GRP hull in excess of the Lloyd's specified thickness, but neglected to add the stiffeners called for later in the same section. Even sillier is 'Moulded in a Lloyd's Approved shop' — Lloyd's Register doesn't 'approve' workshops, only *accepting* them as suitable environments in which to build boats to their rules.

If a vessel is built to a classification society's standards, then it will have some form of certification confirming this. If in doubt as a potential purchaser, ask to see it. If for any reason it cannot be produced, ask the classification society.

A jaunty gaff yawl with topsail set, sails through the anchorage in Studland Bay.

Chapter 12

THE RIG

How or when the first sail developed is unknown. Perhaps some ancient fisherman observed that his billowing cloak lessened his toil as he paddled home for his tea, and then developed his discovery to ease his lot. But we do know that sails go back a long time, featuring in Egyptian wall paintings over 4000 years old. These were simple rigs, using a single square sail with a wooden spar along the top and bottom, and were set only when the wind was favourable to supplement the usual motive power of oars. We know also that the Phoenicians were competent sailors, for whom much credit must be given for very early developments in shipbuilding and navigation, and that they passed on their skills to the Greeks and Romans.

Development languished with the disintegration of the Roman empire. True, the Norsemen were still roaming far and wide in their elegant longships but, although their hulls were superb examples of early naval architecture, their rigs were by contrast very primitive and contributed little to the evolution of sails.

But the concept of free power would not be suppressed. By the 12th century lateen rigged vessels (Figure 7) were trading in the Mediterranean and development was spreading slowly to mariners in north-west Europe. From there on, growth began to accelerate. By the middle of the 15th century ships were becoming larger and having to pile on more sails to produce the drive required. Now the wind was the primary source of power, although oars were still retained in the galleys of the Mediterranean. Trade was becoming inter-continental, and the race to exploit newly discovered territories was calling for bigger and faster ships. Improvements grew apace, achieving glorious culmination in the British and American clippers of the 18th and 19th century.

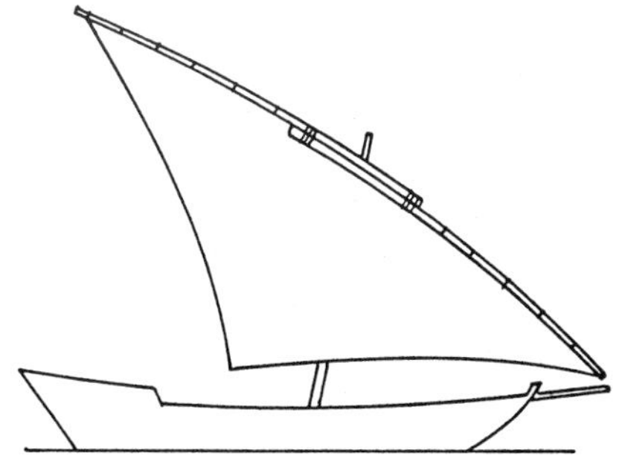

Fig 7. The centuries old lateen rig can still be seen in many parts of the world.

Even to this day, small sailing ships still ply in many parts of the world, offering a vital service to local communities. But the great era of sail has obviously passed into history. The coming of steam killed off the clippers and other commercial sailing ships, the largest which were becoming grotesque anyway. Huge boats require huge sail areas. And simple arithmetic, as well as advancing technology, was against them. For, whilst volume (and therefore cargo carrying capacity) increases by the cube, sail area only increases by the square. The largest vessels simply couldn't carry enough sail to propel the weight they bore, despite resorting to extreme rigs with six or seven masts.

For the origins of the modern yacht rig we must look towards the Dutch, who were the first to develop the fore-and-aft mainsail more or less as we know it today. Indeed the word 'yacht' itself stems from the early Dutch *jaght-schip* of the 17th Century. By the middle of the 18th century, the ease of working and the good windward performance of such fore-and-aft sail plans had established them firmly amongst the schooners fishing out of Gloucester, Massachusetts, and the numerous different types of fishing boats operating from British and other European ports.

But, whereas the general configuration of the modern yacht's rig might be familiar to our forefathers, today's materials certainly wouldn't. Natural fibres such as flax, cotton, and hemp have yielded to the miracles of modern chemistry. Sailmaking has become a form of engineering.

Most cruising sails are made of polyester cloth, very tightly woven and treated with a resin filler to improve their dimensional stability. The exceptions are **spinnakers** and other downwind sails, which are usually made of nylon. Racing yachts (and some exotic cruisers) carry sails made of very high-strength fibres (such as Kevlar) or of laminated plastic films (Mylar), providing even better low-stretch qualities and resistance to deformation. However, these sails are expensive, awkward to handle and stow, and often have a short life due to degradation by sunlight.

Ropes, too, have been transformed, both in strength and 'feel'. The smooth, supple rope of today is in all ways superior to the stiff, hairy coils that yachtsmen were obliged to wrestle with until as recently as the sixties.

Similarly, heavy timber spars have been replaced by extruded aluminium alloy. The **standing rigging** (the shrouds and stays which support the mast) is now almost always of stainless steel wire. The whole rig in its entirety is much stronger, lighter, and so much easier to maintain.

Sails should not be thought of simply as bags of air, to be blown along in the manner of an autumn leaf. They are carefully designed aerofoils having much in common with an aircraft's wing. As the air flow passes over them (Figure 8), the air pressure becomes lower on the convex side, generating an imbalance of pressures which literally *sucks* the sail forward. As can be seen from the diagram, the resultant **lift** of these combined forces is at an angle to the direction of travel. As well as the forward drive component, there is also a fair amount of sideways pull which accounts for both the heeling effect and leeway.

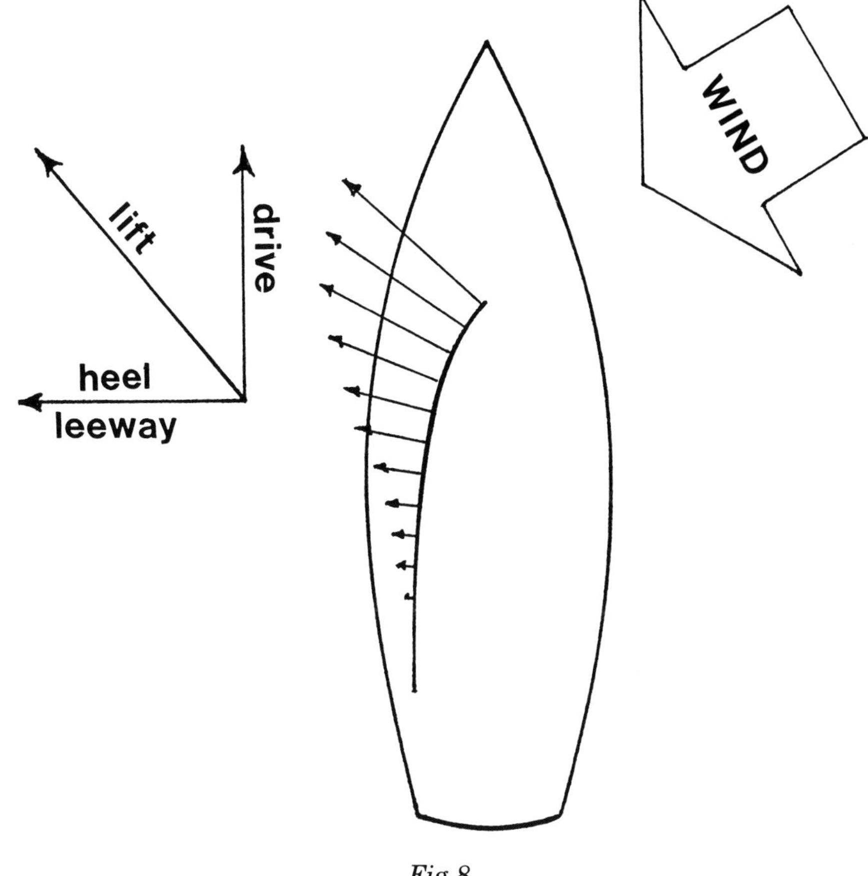

Fig 8

The shape of the sails is critical for different conditions and it is beholden upon the crew to **trim** (adjust) them optimally to get the best performance for every point of sailing. The skill with which this is done is perhaps the most important distinction that sets the expert crew apart. Unfortunately, without the competitive edge of racing, with its continuous boat-for-boat comparisons, it is an art which many cruising yachtsmen never fully master.

Before we move on to the different types of rigs, perhaps it would be timely to unravel some of the jargon surrounding this subject.

Bermudan mainsail: A triangular fore-and-aft sail whose **luff** (forward edge) runs up a track on the aft side of the mast, and whose **foot** (bottom edge) is attached to a horizontal spar called a **boom.**

Gaff mainsail: Similar to the above but quadrilateral in shape. The upper edge of the sail is laced to a spar called a **gaff.** Sometimes, but not usually, gaff sails are set **loose footed,** which means there is no boom.

Headsail: Any triangular fore-and-aft sail set forward of the mast.

Jib: A small headsail. Jibs can either be hanked to the **forestay** or set **flying,** which means it is simply attached to the vessel by its three corners. A **storm jib** is an especially heavy sail for use in the most severe conditions.

Genoa: A larger headsail, at least partially overlapping the mainsail. Genoas are only rarely set flying as this would make them very difficult to handle. In many cruising yachts the genoa is fitted to a **reefing gear** which allows it to be rolled up to reduce the area as the wind increases.

Mizzen: A sail similar to the mainsail but set on the aft-most mast of a yacht with more than one mast. Mizzens can either be bermudan or gaff, though the former is now much more common.

Mizzen staysail: Similar to the jib, but set from the mizzen mast.

Spinnaker: A large ballooning sail, roughly triangular and symmetrical in shape — the only non-fore-and-aft sail usually carried on a modern cruising yacht. Spinnakers are always set flying and are trimmed with the aid of a **spinnaker pole** to hold the sail open. Increasingly popular are cruising derivatives of the spinnaker — asymmetrical sails variously called *cruising chutes, coasters, gennikers,* depending upon the sailmaker. These are somewhat easier for a short-handed crew to handle and can often be flown without a pole.

Storm trysail: A small triangular sail made of very heavy cloth which is set in place of the mainsail in the most severe conditions.

At this stage it might be worth talking about **balance.** This has nothing to do with the ability of a sailboat to stay upright, but describes the tendency of a boat either to **round up** (turn) towards the direction from which the wind is blowing or to **bear away** which is the opposite. A boat which rounds up is said to have **weather helm,** because you need to pull the tiller to weather (windward) in order to correct it. A boat which bears away is said to have **lee helm.**

A small degree of weather helm is usually considered desirable — not least because if the helmsman is incapacitated (or, God forbid, falls overboard), the boat will come up head-to-wind and stop. In a well designed sailboat this can be achieved by adjustment of the sails, but some boats are just inherently badly balanced and there is little you can do — particularly in strong conditions when the boat is heeled over — to trim out the weather or lee helm.

Sails are the raiments of yachts and, as such, are perhaps the most vivid expression of a boat's character. Very often a particular rig is chosen because it looks 'pretty' or 'nautical', without regard to its efficiency or suitability. Designers are often to blame for they know what appeals and aren't above gilding an otherwise honest lily to increase sales. But what looks good on a drawing may be awful at sea. In reality *simple* is nearly always beautiful!

And now to the most commonly seen rigs.

Sloop: Another word from the Dutch — *sloep.* This is overwhelmingly the most popular rig for small to mid-sized yacht, and for the very good reasons. A single mast carries a mainsail and one headsail (at a time). The sloop rig is very efficient upwind and offers a valuable combination of performance versatility and supreme simplicity.

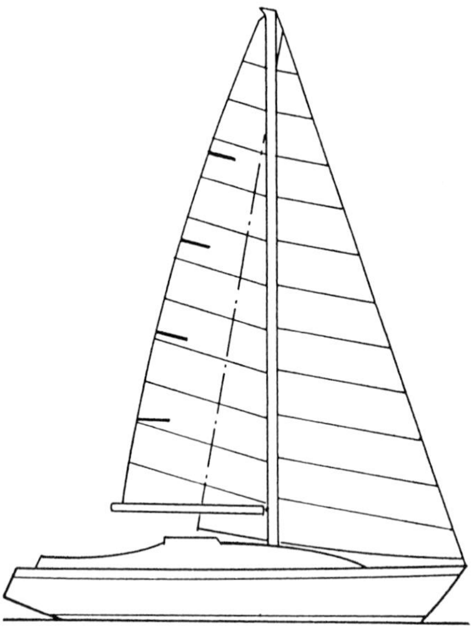

Fig 9. A modern Bermudan sloop.

Variations include the **masthead sloop** (where the forestay attaches to the top of the mast) and the **fractional sloop** (where the forestay is attached at a point below the top of the mast). The latter type is more usually found in pure racing boats or cruiser/racers. Unless there are good reasons to the contrary, the sloop should be everyone's first choice.

Cutter: Similar to the sloop but carrying two headsails, the inner of which is set on an inner forestay and is called a **staysail.** The mast on a cutter is often stepped further aft than on a sloop. This rig is favoured by some long distance yachtsmen, who like the security of the extra standing rigging, and the ability to set a **storm jib** on the more easily accessible inner forestay. The extra work entailed in having to tack two headsails instead of one is of less importance on long voyages, but can be arduous in restricted waters with frequent changes in course. The cutter is not as efficient as a sloop upwind, but is a powerful and easily balanced combination when **reaching** (sailing with the wind on or about abeam).

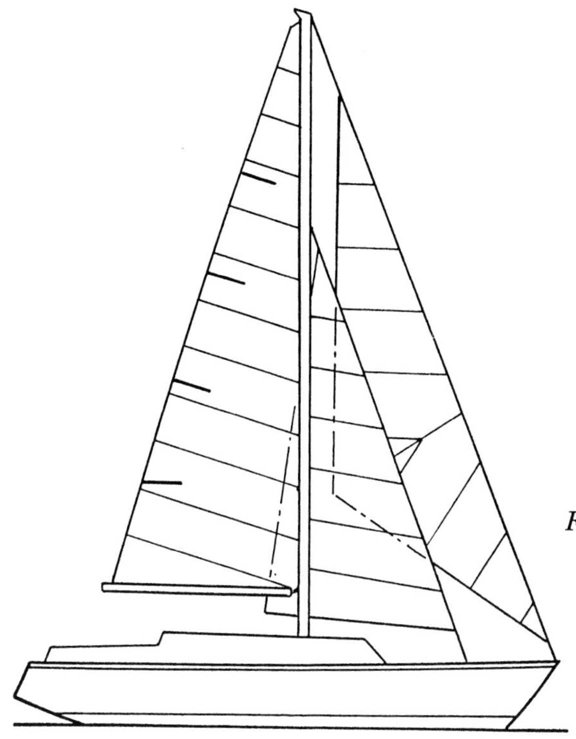

Fig 10. A bermudan cutter.

Ketch: A two-masted rig, with a tall main mast forward and a shorter mizzen mast aft — popular for its 'big boat' look. Enthusiasts claim that because the total sail area is divided between two masts, each individual sail is smaller and therefore lighter to handle. Whilst obviously significant on larger yachts, this argument seems somewhat irrelevant for smaller vessels where even the heaviest sail is easily managed. The ketch is a good reaching rig but performs less well upwind — a point of sailing where the mizzen becomes virtually useless. Most small ketches would have made better sloops or cutters, but the rig does come into its own as length increases.

Incidentally, a **yawl** (from the Scandinavian *yol*) is in appearance very similar to a ketch. But here the mizzen is stepped further aft — sometimes almost right on the stern. Not many yawls are built these days.

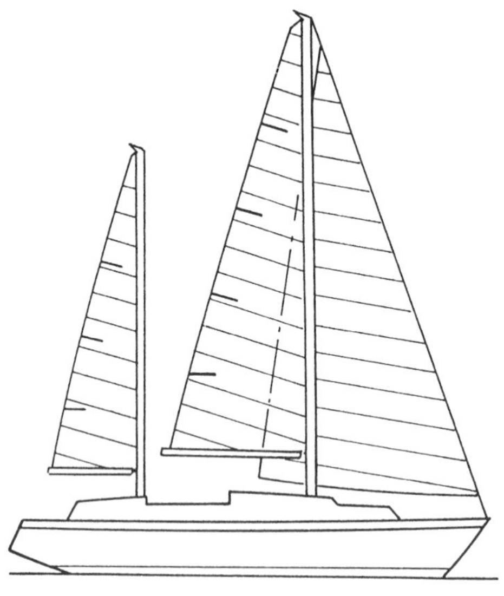

Fig 11. A modern ketch with bermudan mainsail

Schooner: Another two-masted (or more) rig, one where the masts are either of equal height or the forward one is shorter. Similarly to the ketch, this rig is really better suited to larger yachts. Small schooners make very little sense.

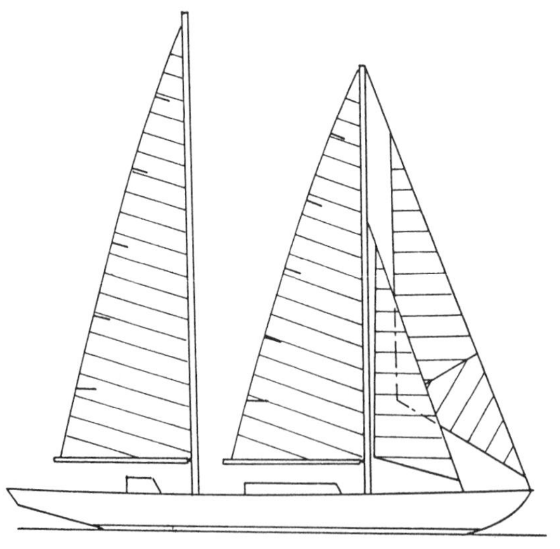

Fig 12. A schooner.

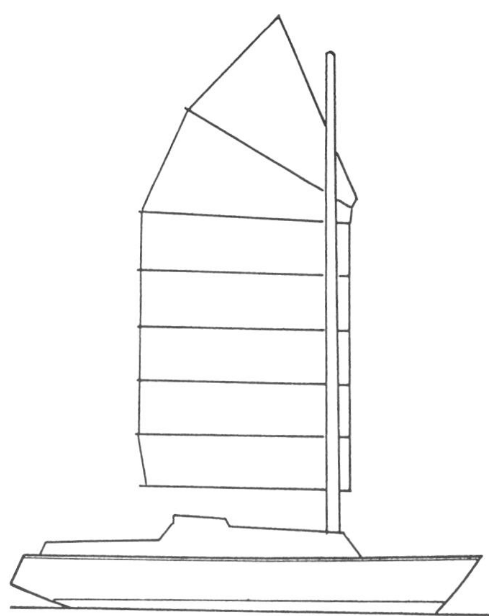

Fig 13. The junk or Chinese lugsail rig

Junk Rig: More correctly described as a Chinese lugsail rig. The sails are visually very distinctive and rely on full-length **battens** to maintain their curious fan-like shape. The masts are usually **unstayed** (not supported by any standing rigging) and, therefore, must be stout enough to resist the side loads unaided. No headsails are carried.

The main virtue of this rig is that it can be reefed from the cockpit by lowering the sail a panel at a time, rather in the manner of a venetian blind. However, it is a very poor performer, particularly to windward and in light conditions where the inability to increase sail area by setting large headsails is most acutely felt.

Freedom Rig: Designed by Gary Hoyt, this rig also has free-standing masts and usually carries no headsails. The original versions had 'wrap-around' sails and **wishbone** booms which sometimes proved difficult to lower due to the friction. Later models run the sails up tracks, in the same way as most other modern yachts (making them, perhaps more correctly, **cat rigged** in the sailing terminology of the United States). Easy tacking is this rig's most conspicuous strength but, like the junk, it has difficulty setting light weather sails and isn't very efficient to windward.

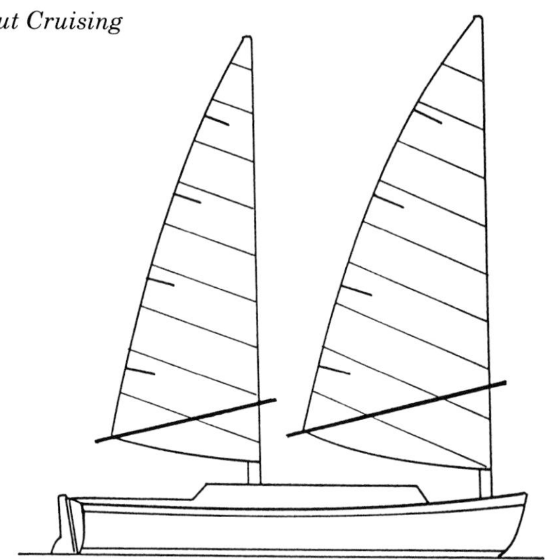

Fig14. A 'Freedom' *rigged ketch.*

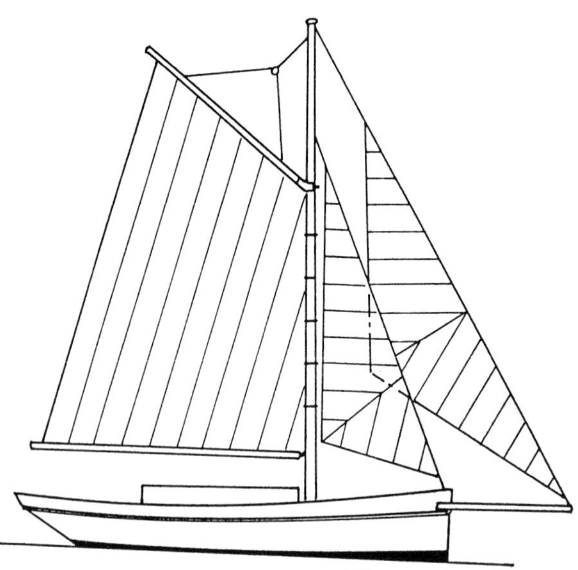

Fig 15. A gaff cutter of traditional type

Gaff Rig: This is somewhat misleading as it describes a specific kind of mainsail or mizzen and not an entire rig at all. These days the gaff rig is only found on older types of boats, whether actually old or modern replicas of traditional types. The gaff rigged sail can feature in a variety of configurations: For instance, you can have a gaff rigged sloop, cutter, ketch or schooner. This is a heavy rig (especially aloft where you don't really want extra weight) which has few advantages other than visual quaintness.

Reefing:

Whatever the rig, the ability to adjust its area to suit the prevailing conditions is vital — and the easier and more safely this can be accomplished the better. Reefing can either be achieved by changing actual sails for ones of different size — say, lowering the genoa when the wind pipes up and setting a smaller jib in its place — or by some means of altering the area of each sail without removing it entirely.

Mainsail reefing has been with us for years. The simplest method is now known as **slab reefing** (a development of what was once called **point reefing**) and involves partially lowering the sail and taking up the slack by lashing the **bunt** (loose, gathered area) to the boom. Another system involves mechanically rotating the boom, thus rolling the sail onto it, with a further modern refinement using an internal spindle which actually winds the sail into the boom's *interior,* rather as a film might be wound into a cassette. Similar to this last arrangement, but operating around a vertical axis, are systems which wind the sail into the mast — commonly known as **in-mast** systems. In my opinion, this type is potentially dangerous as you would have no means of lowering the mainsail should the gear jam. Also, the weight of the mainsail remains permanently aloft, even when fully furled.

Slab reefing is the most reliable and the least expensive. If properly arranged, it can be speedily executed, without too much exposure for the crew. But the other methods do offer some extra convenience which might be especially attractive in bigger yachts where mainsail areas are large.

But, whereas the potential vulnerability of mechanical mainsail reefing systems has as yet created only tepid enthusiasm amongst cruising yachtsmen, the genoa reefing gear has been widely embraced. Here the genoa is rolled around an aluminium section which rotates around the forestay. Winding power is provided by a line and drum assembly at the tack (or, in larger boats, by hydraulic or electric motors). The aerodynamic efficiency of the partially furled genoa isn't quite as good as an individual sail of that size, but sailmakers are continuously improving the way they set. Many people feel that any marginal losses in performance are more than compensated for by the safety gained in not having to send a crew member onto the foredeck, perhaps in awful conditions. Another great advantage is that because a single roller furling genoa will do the work of many different sized headsails, you don't have all those extra sail-bags cluttering up the accommodation. Incidentally, unlike in-mast mainsail reefing systems, should a genoa reefing gear seize in service, the sail can usually still be lowered by first unwinding it by hand from around the forestay.

Some rigs are just downright awesome. Creole, *a 190′ (58m) three masted schooner, flies the largest spinnaker I have ever seen.*

Chapter 13
THE GEAR

As many people have found, quite literally to their cost, the spending doesn't stop when you've first acquired your sailboat. It's true that second-hand boats sometimes change hands with most of their working gear aboard, but the chances are that much of it will be worn out and will require early replacement. New boats, on the other hand, are usually delivered with an inventory so meagre that they are barely fit to lie alongside in the marina — let alone put to sea. Some even come without sails!

Most yacht surveyors have experienced boarding some gleaming creation to find the lockers devoid of equipment. A tiny anchor is stowed in the forepeak, the mooring lines are too short, and there are no lifejackets, safety harnesses, flares, or even fire extinguishers aboard. All too often the owner has stretched his funds to buy the biggest yacht he can, without budgeting for the inevitable shopping list of essential extras. And now he is the proud owner of a boat he can hardly use — very often the reason that it's back on the market so quickly.

So, it's vital that we be truly realistic about this. If the price of a boat leaves you too financially strapped to fit it out properly, then look for a less expensive boat. Much more than comfort and convenience is involved; one day your life may depend upon it.

PERSONAL GEAR

A common introduction to sailing is to crew on somebody else's boat. Many years ago, I was occupying my usual position in the yacht club bar when a friend introduced me to a new member — a young man with a recent beard and intensely eager expression. Desperate for a berth, I was told. Ready and willing but with nowhere to go. He had heard I was setting off alone for Cherbourg next day and just wondered....?

Well, he seemed an agreeable enough fellow so I agreed. Next morning he appeared at the dock, grinning ecstatically and clutching his crew-bag.

'Got everything you need?' I asked.

He nodded and jumped aboard.

Everything went fine until about mid-Channel. It was early summer and none too warm. A small depression to the west had deepened and the wind was picking up. I knew it wasn't anything very serious but it could get messy. Sure enough, an hour later rain began speckling the decks. Light spray was being lifted over the weather rail and I could feel the wind biting through my sweater.

'Go below and put on your oilskins' I told my young friend.

He stared at me blankly for a few seconds before disappearing down the hatch. I could hear him drag out his bag and draw back the zipper. A few minutes later he emerged wearing a hairy sports coat, a tweed cap, pigskin gloves and a very sheepish expression.

'Going to the races?' I asked, and he blushed like a schoolgirl.

Luckily, I had an old set of oilskins aboard so was soon able to deck him out in a manner more appropriate to the situation. But for both him and me it was a valuable lesson. Even if he had been prepared to tough it out, it would have been only a matter of time before he would have had to go below. For, once wet, even in quite mild climates, heat loss through water evaporation and wind chill can quickly incapacitate a man to the point where he becomes a burden to his fellow crew members and a possible danger to himself. Symptoms of exposure appear well before the actual survival threshold, and further down that chilly road is the horror of hypothermia which can ultimately lead to death. Any sensible skipper simply musn't allow that to happen, and I — as I've often since reminded myself — should have taken the trouble to check.

But although it remains the ultimate responsibility of the skipper to ensure that his crew is properly equipped, it's not up to him to actually provide the gear for you.

Wet-weather Gear: 'Oilies', 'foulies', 'slickers', 'weathers', whatever you care to call them, these are probably the most important items in a cruising yachtsman's kit. Most manufacturers market a comprehensive range, extending from the lightweight, relatively inexpensive suits for the occasional sailor, to those offering the kind of protection you would need off Cape Horn. Obviously, there is a wide spread in price, quality, and the specific features of each type of garment.

Typically, a set of oilskins comprises a jacket and trousers. The jacket can be either of the smock type, which you pull on over your head, or with zips or buttons down the front. Oilskin jackets usually have an integral hood — often folded into the collar when not in use.

Trousers can either have an elasticated waist or be 'high-waisted', where they extend upwards almost to the armpits and are supported by shoulder straps. A front opening is often provided for the convenience of men. Ladies, with their internal plumbing, aren't so lucky.

It would be nice to sail like this always, but sometimes conditions will demand better protection.

The quality and durability of materials also varies. At the lower end of the scale you have reinforced PVC — shiny and often yellow — and at the most expensive end close-weaved nylon, internally waterproofed with a polyurethane coating. In between there is a selection of other fabrics. These include very lightweight nylons (useful for shower protection or use in the tropics) and some that are micro-porous, to allow water vapour from perspiration out without allowing rain or sea water in.

Obviously the prime function of wet weather gear is to keep you dry. In this regard there have been great advances over the years. Manufacturers have been very ingenious in devising new tricks to keep the water at bay. Internally taped seams, special cuffs, double flaps over closures and pockets — all contribute to this vital defence. But, again, there is a correlation between cost and efficacy. The more sophisticated the garment, the more you will have to pay for it.

If cruising in higher latitudes, you will also be looking for warmth. Some oilskins have permanent insulation built in, but this can be both limiting and awkward. A suit made especially for me for the Round Britain Race was so heavily padded I waddled around the boat like some fat robot, deliciously warm but almost totally immobilised. A better idea is the removable insulated liner or, as favoured by some manufacturers, an entire system of clothing which is donned in layers from the skin outwards. Versatility is important. To be able to use the same gear in winter or in summer is a great boon.

Better quality oilies can offer additional features. These could include partial flotation, full flotation in the form of an inflatable lung, built in safety harness, and reflective tape flashes and strobe lights in case you fall overboard.

An unfortunate development in the design of wet weather gear has been the encroachment of the 'stylist'. Obviously a natty appearance helps sales but, should a crew member be lost over the side, some of the colour combinations may not be very easy to spot amongst the waves. It's worth bearing this in mind when you make your choice.

Safety Harness: As vital to your safety as oilies are to your comfort. Most harnesses are made up of nylon or polyester webbing which passes around your chest and over your shoulders. A short length of rope tethers you to any secure anchorage on your boat. Most prudent skippers insist on a harness being worn when working the foredeck in brisk weather, and at all times for the watch on deck at night.

It's particularly important that you have your own harness as they must be adjusted to fit the individual, and this can't be done in a hurry. Ideally, it should be conspicuously marked so that you can identify it instantly. It's also not sufficient to rely on the harness which may be built into your oilskin jacket. In hot weather a harness could be the *only* thing you may want to wear!

Again, quality varies, and it's worth paying for the best. Be wary of the **carbine hook** (clip) at the end of the tether. Some can spontaneously unclip if pulled from certain angles — not a reassuring thought when your life may depend upon it. The better types have a latch which positively locks them closed.

Also, some harnesses are much easier to put on than others. I've seen intelligent men reduced to impotent, gibbering rage, trying to work out which arm goes through where. Imagine having to do it in the dark.

Lifejacket: This is another vital bit of gear which, although often part of a yacht's permanent inventory, is worth owning yourself.

Modern lifejackets fall broadly into two categories: inflatable and non-inflatable. The latter type is usually filled with kapok or a closed-cell plastic foam and is considered safer as it will continue to support you even if punctured. However, they tend to be rather bulky for use on a small boat and most yachtsmen (myself included) prefer the inflatable variety, which can be worn deflated until required.

Of these there are sub-species. The most basic is simply inflated by mouth. Slightly more refined are those with a small CO_2 gas cartridge which can be activated instantly by squeezing a trigger or tugging at a lanyard. The most sophisticated (and expensive) inflate automatically when a sensor is immersed in water long enough to know that it hasn't just been splashed with spray — useful if a crew member is stunned as he falls overboard. Some hybrid designs have a degree of permanent buoyancy, which is augmented by inflation should the need arise. Nearly all are equipped with whistles, and some with flashing lights to assist the search.

Many different countries have official agencies which control and certify that prescribed standards of design, manufacture, and performance efficacy are achieved. These standards invariably insist upon a minimum amount of buoyancy, disposed in such a way as to automatically turn an unconscious person onto his back, and then to support his head above water to prevent him drowning. Before buying a particular lifejacket, it is worthwhile checking that it carries the endorsement of such an authority.

It is important to note that **buoyancy aids,** as worn by water skiers, sailboarders, etc., are *not* lifejackets and have no place on a cruising yacht. They are fine for general watersports but do not necessarily have all the features required.

Deck Shoes & Boots: Contrary to popular belief, the non-slip qualities of bare feet are poor — especially on a wet teak deck. Deck shoes are more than vanities, to be worn for posing in yachty fashion in your waterfront bar; they are an important part of your personal kit and should be chosen with care.

As always, quality counts. The best have soles made of special compounds, formed in such a way as to maximise grip. Uppers can either be leather or fabric but must be treated so as not to be destroyed by the sea water.

Whereas having wet feet might be refreshing on a hot summer's day, it can be absolute misery during a cold night watch. Rubber sailing boots (yellow wellies) are, therefore, also essential, and should be bought large enough to wear with thick socks beneath.

Other items are also worth including in your crew bag. A towelling scarf is wonderful for stemming those malevolent little trickles that always seem to find their way down the back of your neck. Thermal underwear is a joy when the temperature drops — sailing gloves or mittens likewise. In high summer or the tropics a pair of light cotton pyjamas will be both cool and protective against the ferocity of the sun. Sunglasses — preferably the 'sports' type, designed for high glare conditions — are also a must.

DECK GEAR:

This topic alone could be the subject of a whole book. The numerous bits and pieces that go to make up any yacht's equipment are legion, and it would be beyond the compass of a single chapter to embrace them all in detail. Therefore I have assumed that the builder has gone about his business in a conscientious way, and that the basic items are already aboard: mast stepped and rigged; rails and lifelines of adequate height and secure; and sufficient cleats, lead blocks and other fittings necessary to handle the boat at sea under sail or power, and to moor it alongside when you come into port. I have also ignored many of the smaller things you will need such as mooring lines, fenders, buckets, and all the other odds and ends that go to make up a cruising yacht's inventory. Instead I have concentrated on the major elective items, which will deserve detailed consideration in selection and budgeting.

Winches: The 'muscle' of the modern sailboat, used for hauling in the various ropes utilised in sail handling. The simplest have no internal gearing and rely upon the length of the winch handle to obtain mechanical advantage. Obviously there is a practical limit as to how long a handle can be (10" (25.4cm) is usually the maximum), so gears are used to increase the power output. Some geared winches are **single speed,** others are **two speed** (with a high and low gear) and, at the top of the rung are the **three speed** winches, usually only found in larger yachts.

The choice of winch should be tailored around the task expected of it. It goes without saying that enough power should be provided to do the job, but too much power can be detrimental as the low gearing will mean very slow winding speeds. Nonetheless, it's better to err on the generous side. Remember the weakest member of the crew.

Sails: I know this was covered in the previous chapter, but a further point should be made. No matter how prudent the skipper might be, sailboats can be caught out unexpectedly in any kind of weather, and it's necessary to have *all* the sails aboard to cope with anything that may arise. In addition to the working canvas, the cruising sailboat should carry a **storm jib** (and, ideally, though less commonly a **storm trysail**) which can be set independently of any roller reefing gear. Also, light weather sails such as spinnakers, cruising chutes, and light genoas are a real advantage when the breeze falls away.

Even if a spinnaker is not carried, a spinnaker (or **whisker** — somewhat lighter) pole will prove invaluable in controlling the genoa when sailing downwind **wing and wing** (with the mainsail set one side of the boat and the genoa the other).

Ground Tackle: In some respects your anchor and chain can be regarded as a sort of maritime hand-brake, to be applied when you fancy stopping for a while. But it can also be much more than this, as we once found when anchored in Cala de Fornells, an attractive and well protected little bay on the north shore of the Mediterranean island of Menorca.

A good meal ashore, with a fairish wine, was spent in company with the crew of another yacht. After we had eaten we carried our drinks out onto the restaurant's terrace. Before us the water lay as heavy and dark as a pool of ink, stretching to where our boats floated motionless above their own reflections. It was one of those glorious summer nights, where no one dare speak above a whisper. Later, as we rowed across the bay, the wake from our dinghy seemed almost a violation.

Now, Chele and I have an agreement when at anchor. If either of us awakes at night, it's a small matter to take a turn around the deck to make sure everything's in order. On that particular night Chele woke just before daybreak. I think I was already dimly aware that the wind had picked up but was in no mood to stir. I heard her climb the companionway and stumble half asleep into the cockpit.

For the purposes of family history, our recollection of the next few seconds differs. Chele claims she said 'Oh phooey (sic!), I do believe we're dragging' or words in a similar mild vein. But I seem to recall a piercing shriek followed by much pounding of the cabin top and some voluble encouragement to get my rear end up there fast. Either way, I tumbled out of my bunk pretty quickly to find we were within a few yards of some exceedingly hostile looking rocks. Drugged by good food and perhaps too much wine, our sailors' sense of danger had failed to notify us of the arrival of a *tramontana,* the spiteful northerly gale that regularly comes rolling down from the Gulf de Lyons to pound that area. The wind was blowing fit to bust and our anchor was bouncing along the bottom of the bay as merrily as a child's ball.

We had the engine started and were out of trouble within seconds, but it took hours for the fright to subside. It had been my fault entirely. Too lazy to haul out *Big Momma,* our hefty working anchor, I had elected to use a dainty little 'lunch hook' which had obviously been far too puny for the unexpected gale.

Good and generously sized ground tackle can often be your last line of defence when threatened off a weather shore. More boats are lost driven ashore than ever are sunk in open water. The land, not the sea, is the sailor's enemy — and anything that keeps him off it has got to be worth the money. Anchor manufacturers compete technically with one other — each claiming their own brand to be superior. I believe that sometimes, no doubt in good faith, they overstate their product's effectiveness. For example, a typical brochure I have before me tells me that for a 33 ft' (10.06m) cruising yacht a 22 lb (10 kg) anchor is sufficient. Experience tells me this is nonsense. For coastal cruising at least a 35 lb (16 kg) anchor should be carried, and for long distance cruising, when you might need to ride out a hurricane, a 70 lb (31.8 kg) anchor would be appropriate.

Different designs of anchor suit different bottom conditions. An anchor which works well in mud may be less effective on hard sand or shingle. Ask around and see what type is favoured in your locality. If travelling further afield, carry a selection. *Spook* carries four — a Bruce, a Delta, a Sea-claw and a traditional fishermens' type, in a range of sizes. Some might judge that excessive, but, when you're clinging by your fingernails to the edge of things, it's nice to know they are equal to the task.

The anchor warp may be either of chain or nylon rope. If the latter, then a short length of chain (usually about 20 ft (6.10m) should be inserted between the anchor and the rope to aid the catenary. Chain is the most effective. In reasonable conditions the **scope** (amount let out) should be equal to about three times the depth of water, whereas rope requires at least five.

And, to handle the chain a **windlass** can be useful. Even a fairly heavy anchor can be hauled up by hand when conditions are calm. But when lying to a strong wind or tide it can be quite a struggle. Windlasses on boats below 35 ft (10.67m) LOA are usually manually operated. On larger boats electric or hydraulic windlasses make more sense.

Dinghy: Often referred to as the boat's **tender.** To anchor in some remote spot is one of the most delightful aspects of cruising. Indeed, many would claim that it is the most satisfying part of the whole exercise — the actual sailing being merely soggy interludes between one anchorage and another. And, when you arrive, to be without a dinghy is effectively to be marooned. To be unable to explore ashore, or to join that party gathering promising momentum on a nearby yacht, is to miss half the fun of cruising. Although some people are content to travel from one marina to another — stepping aboard one end, and stepping off at the other — there will always be times when you'll need to anchor, when a dinghy becomes invaluable.

Although some larger and traditional boats may have rigid dinghies, stowed in chocks on deck or inverted on the cabin top, most prefer the inflatable type, of which there are a number of different brands, whose range of prices roughly reflects the considerable spread in quality. All can be propelled by oars and most can be fitted with brackets to take outboard motors.

Another alternative is the folding dinghy, of which various designs exist. These are somewhat quicker to rig than inflatables, and are more like a conventional rigid dinghy to row, but take up more space when stowed.

Windvane Self-steering & Autopilot: In response to a request to take over the tiller, my son Angus once remarked: 'Steering stinks!' He was about ten at the time, and we were making the short passage between the neighbouring West Indian islands of St.Kitts and St.Maartens. A small but vital linkage had broken in the windvane gear and it lay dismantled and useless in the cabin. I had already been at the helm for four hours — an unaccustomed chore aboard a boat which customarily sailed itself. Boredom was mounting, my temper rising. Sensing the onset of some unjustly applied parental authority, Angus beat a safe retreat to the foredeck with his book.

For, although steering can be intensely exhilarating for short periods of time, it can soon become mind-numbingly tedious as hour follows hour. To be freed from the cockpit, and to be able to roam about the boat and enjoy it *as a whole,* is a wonderful liberation. There are also great benefits in being able to use your time on watch engaged in other tasks. Attention to the demands of navigation and keeping a look-out can be so much more attentive when your eyes are not glued to the compass, and your hand not gripping a tiller or wheel. Personally, I wouldn't have a boat which could not be made to self-steer.

Self-steering gears fall into two distinct categories, with various sub-species of both types.

The first type is entirely mechanical and is commonly called a **windvane gear** or sometimes simply a **vane gear.** These were first developed for model sailboats and later adapted for full-size yachts by a number of people, most notably 'Blondie' Hasler who, as we mentioned earlier, was one of the instigators of the Singlehanded Trans-Atlantic Race. A vane senses changes in the apparent wind direction (much in the manner of a weathercock) as the boat yaws off course and, through a series of linkages, transmits a corrective movement either to the main rudder or to a smaller auxiliary rudder. Because the initiating power from the vane is quite feeble, most gears use some means of mechanical amplification to enhance their effect. The most powerful types, called **pendulum servo gears,** actually harness the water flow past the hull to exert the necessary forces on the tiller.

Windvanes work well when the apparent wind is strong enough, but tend to be less efficient in light conditions or when running downwind (when the boat's own speed actually detracts from the windspeed). Because they are *wind sensing,* they obviously do not hold the sailboat on a compass course, but will follow the windshifts wherever they may blow. Therefore a weather eye on the compass is always prudent.

The second type is the **electronic autopilot** which, as its name implies, runs on electricity from the yacht's batteries. Yacht autopilots are the smaller cousins of the sophisticated units which guide commercial craft, and share many of the same features. Falling prices and the sheer convenience of autopilots have made them increasingly popular. And this trend is likely to continue.

Although some may have wind sensing as an option, most electronic autopilots use integral **fluxgate compasses** for directional reference. This type of compass senses the earth's magnetic field without using a needle or other moving part. The most complex autopilots will also interface with other navigational systems and can be programmed to perform a number of useful tricks — for instance, to steer the boat to a specific point on the chart (a **waypoint**), compensating as it goes for the influences of wind and tide.

On the face of it electronic autopilots would seem to have it hands down over windvane gears but, as usual, there's a snag. They are electrically thirsty beasts, and the drain on the batteries is often beyond the rate of replenishment on smaller sailboats. I once arrived unerringly at Gibraltar to find the batteries so depleted I had to crank start the diesel by hand — not always possible on some models.

Long distance sailors tend to rely on windvanes, whilst the electronic autopilot's simplicity of operation is ideal for shorter hops where going in and out of marinas usually keeps the batteries in a good state of charge. The best arrangement, of course, would be to carry both — the windvane for use when there is wind, and the autopilot for use under power (perhaps in calm conditions) when the engine would be supplying ample electricity.

A vane gear can release you from the tedium of steering. This trim-tab gear on Spook was made with simple tools and works well on most points of sailing.

ELECTRONIC INSTRUMENTS:

The proliferation of electronic gadgetry has been truly astonishing over the past few years. Thirty years ago, when I was serving as a young officer in the Merchant Navy, not even the great ocean liners could boast the kind of electronic wizardry seen on quite modest yachts today. The development of the microchip has penetrated sailing as deeply as it has life ashore. Whether or not this trend is altogether to the good is open to debate, but certainly it will not only endure but accelerate. Often, for us veterans of a simpler era, the main problem is just keeping abreast with these impressive advances.

Depth Sounder: Also commonly called an **echo sounder** because this describes the principle on which it works. A high frequency sound signal is emitted in regular pulses from a **transducer** beneath the hull, and the same transducer receives the echo as it bounces back from the bottom of the sea. As the speed of sound through water is known, the interval between the transmission of the signal and the return of the echo gives an accurate indication of the depth beneath the boat.

Added features of some depth sounders include: a shallow water alarm, which will sound a buzzer when the boat strays into water less than a pre-set depth; and an anchor alarm which sounds the same buzzer if the depth of water changes suddenly.

Log: To measure speed, our ancient mariner would toss a piece of wood (hence 'log') from the bow and measure the time it took to sweep down the side of his ship. In a later refinement, a rope with knots spaced along it was attached to the log, and the number of knots counted as it streamed astern for a set period of time. The **knot** still remains our unit of speed — one knot being a *nautical* mile (of 6076.12 ft or 1852m) per hour.

Simple mechanical logs can still provide the modern navigator with the information he needs. These count the turns of a specially designed **rotator,** towed on a line astern, which are counted and translated into distance covered.

Modern instruments operate similarly, but electrically count the turns of a tiny impeller or paddle wheel, which protrudes through a special retractable fitting in the bottom of the boat. This information is typically expressed as both speed (in knots) and distance run (in nautical miles).

It should be noted that logs can only measure speed and distance *through the water* and not over the ground. If you were to head directly into a 5 knot current at 5 knots of boat speed you would, of course, be making no headway — but your log would still show 5 knots.

Wind Indicator: These measure *apparent* wind speed and direction. The 'apparent' is important because the yacht's own speed affects the instrument's (and our) perception of from where and how strong the wind is blowing. This is exactly similar to the effects on the log, as we've just discussed. The difference between beating to windward against a strong breeze, and heading downwind in the same conditions is very striking — in one the boat's speed adds to the wind strength, and in the other it detracts from it.

Wind indicators use a pair of sensors built into the same small unit at the top of the mast. One is like a small weathercock (direction) and the other is a set of spinning cups (speed).

Although the depth sounder, log, and wind indicators can be divided between separate instruments — all operating independently — it is becoming increasingly common to see 'integrated' systems driven by a central processor. These systems can not only deal with their own specific functions but can 'trade' information with other compatible units, such as navigational systems and autopilots.

VHF Radio Transceiver: These are the short distance telephones of the marine world, and can be used for boat-to-boat or ship-to-shore communication. Because the radio signal doesn't 'bend' far below the horizon, the range should be considered as more or less 'line of sight' — say, 25 miles maximum.

By international agreement the available channels are allocated for one of six different purposes: distress safety and calling; inter-ship; public correspondence; port operations; ship movement (very similar to port operations); and, in the U.K. only, yacht safety. Additionally, other channels may be approved locally for specific uses — for example, in the U.K. channels M1 and M2 are reserved for communication between yachts and marinas.

Unfortunately, international accord in this matter stops at the United States, where, in their infinite wisdom, they have their own channel frequencies and designated purposes (although some are common to both). Many modern VHF sets can be switched from the International to the US system and vice-versa, but this facility may be internally blocked to prevent you contravening local regulations (transmitting on US frequencies in European waters, for example).

VHF sets on British yachts require a 'Ship Licence' and the operator a 'Certificate of Competence', which is issued after a fairly straightforward examination. This will be covered more fully in Chapter 15.

Radar: Once only found on ships and very large yachts, miniaturisation has made this useful navigational aid a practical proposition for smaller sailboats. Radar (an acronym for *RAdio Detection And Ranging*) was developed during the Second World War to give advance notice of approaching enemy aircraft. In some ways similar to the echo sounder, it works by transmitting micro-wavelength radio signals from a revolving **scanner** (radar aerial), and interpreting the echo to provide an electronic 'picture' of your surroundings on a screen. Obviously, as light is not involved, radar works equally well at night and in poor visibility (though heavy rain can blot it out).

However, some substances reflect radar waves better than others. And small objects (even a yacht) may return such feeble echoes that they can be overlooked. The wry joke about 'radar assisted collisions' is based on grim reality. All too often the faint echo from a small boat can be lost amongst the **clutter** of random echoes from the faces of waves.

And I once inspected a boat which had run ashore in fog because the skipper had mistaken the strong echo from a line of beach-front apartment buildings for the nearly invisible image of the shoreline itself. There had only been a couple of hundred metres in it, but that had been quite enough to put him high on the sand. The yacht club stories about 'how-I-threaded-my-way-into-port-in-a-howling-gale-and-zero-visibility-under-radar-alone' should be considered the admissions of a self confessed fool.

But, despite its limitations, the radar is still a useful bit of kit. Additional features can include interfacing with other navigational systems, and **guard zones** which can be assigned to sound a warning if another vessel enters a prescribed area. On the detrimental side are weight and windage aloft, fairly high electrical drain, and expense.

ELECTRONIC NAVIGATION AIDS:

Micro-chip technology has transformed the way we navigate. But, before we toss away our sextants and chronometers, we should consider this short cautionary tale.

A few years ago I was sailing in the Gulf of Mexico, bound for Tampa in Florida and well out of sight of the Mississippi coast which lay to the north. The weather was perfect; a cloudless sky and a gentle breeze. The vane gear was doing its stuff. My crew and I were pottering around the boat attending to various tasks.

Then, to the south, we saw a large motor yacht travelling at speed on a parallel course. It obviously spotted us at about the same time, for we saw it alter course and head towards us.

Panic! For the Gulf remains a piratical place. The spirit of Captain Morgan lives on in the region. Every year a number of yachts are hijacked and plundered, either for their contents or in order to run drugs into the US mainland. As the motor yacht approached, we broke out the armaments (a regrettable necessity in some waters) and lay them down out of sight in the cockpit.

And then the boat sagged off the plane and was circling us slowly. A loud haler crackled into life.

'Don't get nervous,' it told us, 'I'm not coming closer. My Loran's crapped out. Can you give me course and distance to Biloxi?'

Well, we could and did. After thoughtfully buoying off a six-pack of cold beers for us to retrieve, our motor yacht was on its way again, throwing up a huge plume of spray.

The moral of this story is plain. Electronic equipment, though miraculous in operation, is also very fallible. It only takes a tiny drop of water to incapacitate a whole system, and repair is usually impossible at sea. Ironically, on that occasion we hadn't had Loran aboard, and were navigating in the time-honoured manner by **dead-reckoning** (chart work) and sights of the sun and stars.

So, although electronic systems are valuable navigational aids, they should not be thought of as total substitutes for more laborious, but certainly more reliable, traditional methods.

The systems available divide into two distinct categories: land-based, where the radio transmitters are statically mounted in carefully chosen positions on the earth's surface; and systems based on satellites orbiting above us. All systems require specialised receivers (carried on your boat) to interpret and compare the appropriate transmissions. Positions are usually displayed digitally as **latitude** and **longitude.** With the exception of Omega, the former types function over limited (and usually different) areas. Satellite systems provide world-wide coverage.

Omega: The only land-based system offering world-wide continuous coverage, Omega became fully operational in 1982, when the last of eight transmitters (in Australia) came on stream. In common with Decca and Loran C, Omega compares the time delays in receiving highly accurately transmitted radio pulses to calculate the receiver's position. However, unlike Decca and Loran C, Omega operates on a very low frequency (10-14 kHz), which gives great range at the cost of some loss in accuracy.

Decca: A medium range navigational system which provides coverage in northern European waters, and in north-west and southern Spain. Accuracy is dependent on distance from the transmitters, but is generally very good — within as little as 50 metres if within 50 miles of the transmitters. A characteristic of Decca is its *repeatable* accuracy. That's to say that although readings may differ (within the normal tolerance) between two different boats in the same position, if a boat returns to that position later then the reading on its own Decca set will be the same as the first time it was there. For this reason, Decca is a firm favourite amongst fishermen, divers, and anyone else who might want to accurately relocate an offshore position.

Loran-C: Managed and operated by the US Coast Guard in American waters and by the US Department of Defense elsewhere, Loran-C has a longer range but is somewhat less accurate than Decca. It provides coverage around North America, North Scottish waters, the North Pacific, Saudi Arabia, and much of the Mediterranean. There are no Loran-C chains in the southern hemisphere.

Satnav: The first of the satellite systems, Satnav became available for yachts in about 1980 when suitably low consumption receivers appeared on the market. Five satellites circle the earth on roughly polar orbits at altitudes of about 1075 km., each making a complete circuit in approximately 107 minutes. The earth rotates within the 'bird-cage shape defined by these orbits and, by reference to the satellites, geographical positions can be computed.

Accuracy is good but the wide spacing of the satellites means that periods of up to three hours can elapse between position updates. Therefore, Satnav is more useful for ocean voyaging than coastal work.

Global Positioning System (GPS): The successor to Satnav, this is primarily a military system which (in a slightly degraded form) is available for civilian use.

By 1992 a constellation of twenty-one satellites will be in operation, each orbiting the earth every 12 hours. A minimum of four satellites (the least required for three-dimensional positioning) and a maximum of eight will be 'visible' at any time. Therefore, the system can be considered continuous.

A high degree of accuracy is offered by GPS — within 20 metres under ideal conditions. And as prices for the equipment becomes more and more competitive, it will undoubtedly become the favoured system for both offshore and coastal sailing.

Of course, all developmental advances tend to create obsolescence, and thus it is with navigational systems. GPS will rapidly supersede Satnav, which will be allowed to decay until it becomes unserviceable. The US Government intends to discontinue its control of non-American Loran-C facilities, though it will be offered to the countries concerned for adoption. The outlook for Decca, too, could be limited, although service now seems assured into the next century.

However, there is some reluctance to abandon well established and reliable systems. As GPS is under the control of the US Department of Defense, they retain the capability to disable or limit access to it at any time they choose in order to prevent it being used by enemy forces. This ability to unilaterally shut off an important navigational facility makes other nations understandably nervous. The British Government once favoured the replacement of Decca with Loran-C as the standard back-up system, but the Swedes recently installed new Decca transmitters (and are in no mood to give them up) and Racal (who own Decca) have proposed a new maintenance procedure which makes the future of Decca much more attractive. Also, there is a powerful lobby within the UK from fishermen and other local seafarers who have used Decca for years and rely on its accuracy to lead them to their nets and lobster pots.

No doubt the dust will settle some time in the future but, for now, we're spoiled for choice.

As the full potential of electronics is explored, new devices emerge with bewildering rapidity. Every boat show yields a new crop, ready to amaze. Apart from the equipment we have already discussed, we already have video charts, weather-faxes (which receive meteorological information), and navigational computers which can complete our calculations with blinding speed. And I'm certain we have only just scratched the surface. In the field of electronic navigation aids, truly we ain't seen nothing yet!

But, another word of warning. Navigational aids are just that — *aids!* Because they tend to express their information so neatly packaged, they can easily induce a confidence in their precision that they don't deserve.

A yacht recently went aground on the Plateau des Minquiers — an evil cluster of rocks just south of Jersey in the Channel Islands. The weather was fair and the crew in no immediate danger. They radioed for help, described their predicament, and gave the position displayed on their Decca — a position which puzzlingly placed them in deep water. The duty coastguard questioned this, suggesting that unless the rocks and the pretty yellow buoy were figments of the imagination, perhaps the instrument had skipped a lane. But the skipper remained adamant, repeating the position to the nearest decimal place. 'Okay', sighed the coastguard at last, sensing the futility of further argument, 'we'll come out and get you. But you'll have to wait a while — there's some idiot on the Minquiers we have to rescue first!'

SAFETY EQUIPMENT:

Liferaft: Although there are many accounts of yachtsmen successfully taking to their tenders as their yachts founder beneath them, most dinghies — especially inflatables — cannot seriously be considered as life-rafts because of the length of time they take to deploy and the lack of protection provided.

The dedicated liferaft is basically a doughnut-shaped inflatable with a supported canopy overhead to give shelter from the weather. They are supplied pre-packed by the manufacturers and are contained either in rigid GRP capsules or canvas valises. Survival rations and equipment, to various specifications, are commonly included. Different sizes are available to match the number of crew.

Speed of deployment is obviously vital. With a yacht on fire or badly holed, disaster is only a few moments away. Life-rafts are usually stowed on deck where they can be released in a trice and thrown overboard. Inflation is by a CO_2 cartridge, activated by pulling on a lanyard once the raft is in the water, and takes no more than a few seconds to complete.

Life-rafts are indisputably expensive. Their initial cost is high and they should be serviced and re-packed annually. This expense may be difficult to justify on boats sailing mainly in coastal waters. Many yachtsmen prefer to hire one for that occasional offshore passage.

Lifebuoys: For that most harrowing of marine incidents — a man overboard. Lifebuoys are usually ring or horseshoe-shaped flotation devices which are stowed accessibly on deck — often in quick release brackets on the stern rail. To be entirely effective, they should be accompanied by an attached **danbuoy** (a float with a whip mast and flag) and a flashing light.

Fire Extinguishers: Fire at sea is a terrifying prospect and should be guarded against at all cost. Timber, of course, burns readily. GRP, although difficult to ignite, once alight will continue to burn even below the waterline. Steel boats, although the material itself is non-flammable, are commonly coated with paints which will burn and, anyway, are usually fitted out below with timber. Add to this a few gallons of diesel fuel, a gas cylinder or two, some explosive pyrotechnics, berth cushions that will emit toxic hydrogen cyanide fumes when burned, and you have the makings for an extremely lively situation should it all catch fire.

Marine fire extinguishers fall into three main groups: Dry powder, BCF (Bromo-chloro-diflouro-methane) gas, and foam. All are suitable for electrical and fuel fires and are supplied in various sizes. The BCF type is available in an automatic form which will actuate itself at a pre-determined temperature — ideal for installation in engine compartments, where to open the hatch to fight the flames would admit more combustion-supporting oxygen. However, BCF fumes are dangerous in confined spaces and the crew should be warned accordingly. Dry powder and foam types are entirely safe, though extremely messy in use (though, under the circumstances, it would seem churlish to complain).

Also very useful are fire blankets, commonly used to smother galley fires should they occur.

EPIRB: Another acronym — this time for **Emergency Position Indicating Radio Beacon** — a self-explanatory description. These are small, self-contained, waterproof radio transmitters which can accompany the crew into a liferaft if necessary.

When actuated EPIRBs transmit on international distress frequencies 121.5 Mhz and 243.0 Mhz. These frequencies are continually monitored by a new satellite tracking system as well as all commercial and military aircraft. After receiving an emergency signal, the satellite will beam the information down to a receiving station on the ground. There, by means of a computer, the navigational position of the vessel in distress will be calculated and passed on to the appropriate rescue services. An EPIRB cannot be used for voice communications, and is also incapable of receiving any acknowledgement that help is on its way. But, once you have actually taken to the liferaft, this may be the most valuable piece of kit you have — excepting, of course, the liferaft itself.

Flares: From time immemorial combustion in one form or other has been used to signal distress. To this day 'Flames on the vessel (as from a burning tar barrel)', is specified under Annex IV of the Collision Regulations as a recognised distress signal — though I think you would have to be pretty desperate to resort to such lengths!

A far more convenient visual device is the pyrotechnic flare — a specialised firework intended to draw attention to your plight. Distress flares emit an intense red light and can be either hand-held or rocket. The latter type will project a flare several metres into the air (from where it will descend slowly by parachute) and can be visible for over 25 miles.

A useful daytime distress signal is the **smoke float** which, after ignition, is thrown into the water, whereupon it will give off large amounts of dense orange smoke.

White hand-held flares are also often carried as 'ship-scarers', or for other non-emergency reasons to draw attention to yourself.

Recommendations vary as to the quantity and type of flares you should carry, and are largely dependant upon the intended use of the boat. Manufacturers conveniently market their flares in packs which meet these varying requirements — Inshore, Coastal, Offshore, as well as those complying with specific racing requirements — though these should be thought of as only the *minimum* you should have to hand.

CHARTS & BOOKS:

Recently, for insurance purposes, I was totting up the value of all of the charts, almanacs, nautical tables, cruising guides, and other technical books aboard *Spook,* and was astonished to discover that their total value comfortably exceeded that of all the other navigational gear aboard — including the expensive electronic gizmos.

But they are worth it, every one of them. It seems to me that no matter how much information you have at hand, there are always questions you will fail to answer. Over the years we've collected charts covering the waters we've cruised — often trading with other sailors — and have built up a tidy collection. Some are getting pretty ancient by now (*'Beyond here there be dragons!'*) but the land remains more or less the same shape and, so long as you update the other information (lights, buoys, etc.,) as you go along, they continue to give good service.

Charts: The maps of the sea. British charts are published by the Admiralty Hydrographic Department. They are printed on very high quality paper which will withstand even the kind of diabolical treatment they might receive on a cruising yacht. Over the years some of mine have been copiously marinated in all manner of noxious substances and — although now stained and dog-eared — still continue to be eminently usable.

Most other maritime nations produce their own charts, and the technical standard is generally excellent (though the quality of the paper is sometimes not). In France the Service Hydrographique et Oceanographique de la Marine is responsible for theirs, and nearly all other European countries maintain similar organisations. American charts are produced by the US Hydrographic Department.

Of course all of these are intended primarily for the use of shipping, with an emphasis on the needs of larger vessels. 'Official' charts contain a lot of information of little interest to the average yachtsman and, conversely, because big ships don't go up creeks, often omit some inshore details which might be important. Responding to an obvious market, various commercial publishers have developed ranges of 'yachting' charts designed around the requirements of small boat sailors. These obviously contain all the basic navigational information, but leave out many of the irrelevances and include additional features (chartlets of small harbours and details of suitable yacht anchorages, for instance) usually to a larger scale than the main body of the chart. Often, such yachting charts are brightly coloured so that, for example, differences in depth of water can be seen at a glance. Others are printed on plastic (or sometimes encapsulated in clear plastic envelopes) so that they can be taken on deck into the rain and spray.

Whatever types of charts you have aboard — and most yachts carry a mixture — it's very important that you have *sufficient*. Cover your cruising area comprehensively and in as much detail as you can. You will probably find that this will result in some duplication in coverage but this is infinitely preferable to having 'gaps' which you know little about.

Cruising Guides: Also called **pilot books.** These carry on where the charts leave off, providing even more detailed information on the various ports and anchorages.

But be a little wary. Whereas charts are published by disciplined organisations whose attention to detail and accuracy is meticulous, cruising guides are often the work of a single person or a small team who couldn't possibly be that thorough. Obsolescence overtakes these books rapidly — and in one instance I recall, so rapidly that the guide became obsolete *in advance.*

Chele and I were in the Balearics, lying at anchor off a small town whose houses fringed the curl of a rocky bay. From our cockpit we watched a motor yacht come in from the open sea. It circled the anchorage slowly. Then it went round again, paused, and circled once more. On the flying bridge its owner was looking distraught. He came close by and hailed us.

'Where's the marina?' he asked.

'There isn't one,' we told him.

'Of course there is!' he insisted testily, and waved an open book above his head. 'It says so in this cruising guide. It should be over there!'

Well, as 'over there' was just a jumble of rocks and a tiny beach, he had plainly been misinformed. After he had zoomed off, obviously disgusted, we checked our copy of the same guide. Sure enough, it showed a marina exactly where he had indicated. Obviously, the compiler had anticipated a development which had never materialised — a bold assumption in a land of dedicated procrastinators, where a high proportion of projects never make it past the dreaming stage, let alone reach fruition.

In another occasion we had difficulty finding our way into a Bahamian lagoon because our bang up to date guide showed a prominent water tower which was now nowhere to be seen. We later learned it had been flattened by a hurricane *three years previously!*

But, despite the occasional gaff, cruising guides are a useful part of the navigator's library. They are usually written by sailors, from a sailor's point of view. In addition to the pilotage information, most will give you some insight into the 'flavour' of each place — invaluable when planning your cruise — and will also provide such non-technical (but no less useful) information on local services, interesting excursions ashore, and the best pubs and restaurants in town.

Nautical Almanacs: These are published annually and must therefore be replaced at the start of each season.

The primary function of almanacs is to supply the ephemeral data required for navigation. The positions of the sun, moon, stars, and planets are given for every second of time for celestial (often known as astro-) navigation. The movements of the tides are given on a daily basis for your coastal work.

Lighthouses and buoyage systems for each port are specified in detail and, in this regard, will probably be the most current information you'll have aboard. As your charts will inevitably accumulate errors and omissions as they get older (professional mariners correct them continuously, but this is impracticable for the average yachtsman), this section gives you the opportunity to update your portfolio on a rolling basis as you go along.

Almanacs also cover much the same sort of function as the cruising guides — albeit in terser, less descriptive form. Small chartlets of harbours and anchorages often accompany the buoyage data, so that the information is presented both in text and graphically.

But today's nautical almanac is very much more than a dusty collection of facts. Most are large volumes stuffed with fascinating information on all manner of things *(Reeds,* for instance, even tells you how to go about delivering a baby — a chapter which, mercifully, I've never had need to refer to). If economy is important, and the ship's library is pared to the minimum, it should still be possible to go cruising with nothing more than charts and an almanac aboard.

Other instructional handbooks are available on almost every topic connected with sailing, and these provide very useful sources of reference. No matter how experienced a sailor becomes, sooner or later he will find himself stuck for an answer and, as there is no one else to turn to, will need to look it up in a book. Obviously, the composition of your own library will be a matter of personal choice, but I believe the one aboard *Spook* is fairly typical. Apart from manuals on the specific equipment we use, we also carry general handbooks on navigation, seamanship, meteorology, electrical and engine maintenance, canvas and fancy ropework (for those boring moments), first aid, fishing, cooking, foreign language phrase books, plus various non-specialised tourist guides for the countries we visit.

Chapter 14
THE BUSINESS

Purchase:

Of course there are many ways one can go sailing without actually owning a boat — crewing for others, chartering perhaps — but eventually, if you are truly smitten with the urge, this is unlikely to be enough. There is a tide within the whole process which leads a person inexorably towards ownership. Although cynics might claim it clear proof of mental derangement, others will tell you that the care and maintenance of their own small ship is an important element in the pleasure and fulfilment they gain.

So, how should you go about it and where should you look? In previous chapters we dwelt on the factors that influence choice. By now you should have a fair image of 'the boat most likely to...' though you might still be lacking the essential hands-on experience to confirm your convictions. Nonetheless, that impulse to sniff out the ideal craft must surely be emerging — indeed, it may by now be positively clamouring for satisfaction.

Old or new? — the first question. Let's deal with new first, and sketch out some ideas for further research.

Yachting Magazines: A fruitful area for study. However, it is important to choose your magazines with some care as they tend to specialise — racing, cruising, dinghy sailing, classic boats, multihulls, whatever — though there is a fair amount of overlap in their coverage. A quick flick through the pages will reveal their interests.

These days no one should need warning to be wary of advertisements. The gloss and hyperbole is known to all of us, and our immune systems are probably well able to cope. In the eyes of the copywriter, every boat is the ideal boat, and he is never reluctant to say so in prose often verging on the purple. More measured information can be gleaned from 'boat tests', where editorial staff put a particular boat through its paces and try to comment objectively on performance and other aspects of the design. Other, apparently unrelated articles, can also often provide useful insights into the characteristics of different boats. A well written cruising yarn will sometimes tell you more about the boat than a pile of brochures.

Boat shows offer excellent opportunities to make comparisons.

Boat Shows: These extravagant circuses of the yachting world provide perhaps the best opportunity to judge one boat directly against another. To be able to wander from stand to stand, comparing individual features and variations in quality, can be very enlightening indeed. Ask awkward questions, and don't be too embarrassed to delve into the less accessible areas, casting a critical eye on the workmanship.

And don't be put off by the absurdly snooty attitude one can encounter from some salesmen. It seems a peculiarity of boat shows that many of the people manning the stands seem to pride themselves on sorting the wheat from the chaff — with the vast majority seemingly falling into the latter category. Being baulked by one such individual, who spent the entire period of our brief conversation looking over my shoulder — probably looking out for a 'Fat Cat' with his cigar and mink-clad companion — I came out and asked him how he had so obviously decided that I couldn't afford his boat — a fairly modest one, as it happens. The murmur of support from those waiting behind told me that I wasn't alone in my irritation.

Many builders and agents also offer special boat show 'packages', discounting prices or including extra equipment to promote their wares. Once you've found your boat negotiate hard — it's amazing the deals that can be struck.

Sales Showrooms: Often as potted palmed and piped musicked as their automobile counterparts — the salerooms are obviously dedicated to peddling the particular line of boats carried in stock. But, away from the hurly-burly of boat shows, you should at least have the undivided attention of the sales staff. Your enquiries can be more penetrating and your appraisal of the boat more leisurely. If seriously interested, ask for a trial sail. There will probably be a token charge (to discourage time-wasters) but this is usually refundable on purchase.

Again, haggle without mercy. Especially in the off-season, profits may be sacrificed for cash-flow, and any reasonable offer will be considered. Sometimes demonstration boats are available at substantially below list price.

A friend of mine recently found a boat he liked at the London Boat Show, but after totting up the figures and generally agonising over the matter decided that it was beyond his means. Some days later, the builder telephoned him to tell him that their three month old demonstrator was being replaced. Was he interested?

Certainly interested, but still short of the necessary funds, my friend drove to the saleroom on the Hampshire coast.

'Absolutely loaded,' he was told, after an exhilarating test sail. 'List price a hundred-and-five-thousand, and we're letting it go for ninety...with no commissioning charges.'

My friend gripped his cheque book lest it leapt out and signed itself. Then sanity returned and he sadly shook his head. 'The wife would kill me,' he faltered. 'Can't go a penny over seventy-five thousand.'

He was half way out of the door when a voice behind him said: 'Done!'

But most people start by buying second-hand. Used sailboats usually represent better value for money and often come equipped with many of the extra bits and pieces you will need. Also, it's not quite so intimidating learning through experience when your boat is in less than pristine condition. This is not to say that you will necessarily behave like a student from the Pin-ball School of Seamanship, but you don't have to be a novice to make a mess of coming alongside. Preoccupation with preserving immaculate topsides is going to do nothing for your confidence in the early days. There is reassurance in knowing that a couple of extra scratches amongst so many is hardly going to notice.

Furthermore, although you may think you know exactly what type of boat you want, this view may change with experience. Second-hand boats can usually be bought and sold over shortish periods without a huge depreciation in value. So, even if you make a mistaken choice, you are unlikely to lose too much — you might even make a small profit.

Yacht Brokers: The 'dating agencies' of the yachting world. Unlike boat salerooms, yacht brokers do not normally own the wares they offer, but sell on commission, much in the manner of estate agents or realtors. In Great Britain this commission is typically 8% of the achieved sales value if the vessel is within the country, and 10% if overseas. In the United States and most other countries the commission is 10% across the board. The commission is payable by the vendor, so, as the purchaser, you will pay nothing.

Some brokers cast a wide net, with lists of boats in many areas, even internationally. Others operate more locally, perhaps solely within the confines of a single marina. Certain brokers specialise — in classic boats, or multihulls, for example. Most advertise extensively in the various magazines, so their scope and areas of expertise can be readily determined. Obviously, there's no point in contacting a specialist in maxi-yachts if you're searching for a humble family cruiser.

Although there are some fly-by-night characters around, most yacht brokers are highly professional and will go to considerable lengths to find the boat to suit you. The most reputable will almost certainly belong to a professional organisation — in Britain, the **Association of Brokers and Yacht Agents**, for instance — who lay down qualifications for membership and Codes of Practice which must be strictly adhered to.

When contacting a broker — either personally, or by telephone or letter — you will need to communicate to him the clearest possible definition of the kind of boat you seek. This will include details of suitable type, size, accommodation and — perhaps most importantly price. Remember, no matter how professional a yacht broker might be, he is a salesman at heart, deriving his income from the commission he earns; the more expensive the boat, the more cash he puts in his pocket. Sometimes you can find yourself talking to a broker about boats at around ten-thousand pounds when, unlike the man at the boat show, it becomes apparent that he's decided you can afford fifteen.

Also, bear in mind that the broker may not actually have seen the boat he is selling. He may simply be passing on information given to him by the owner, who, especially if desperate to sell, may not be above a little judicious exaggeration. Find out if the broker has inspected the boat personally. If not, regard anything he might tell you with caution. He won't be lying but he might be ill-informed.

Private Sales: Many owners — most notably of boats in the lower price range — prefer to handle the sale themselves, thus of course saving the broker's commission, though probably incurring some advertising costs. For, the most usual method of putting the word about is by small-ads placed in the classified section of the yachting magazines. Browsing through these cluttered pages can prove useful study for the potential buyer.

Before commencing negotiations, it's worth checking if the saving in brokerage commission is reflected in the asking price. Understandably, vendors want to make as much as possible out of any deal, and may have based their pricing on that of similar boats listed in brokers' advertisements — which, of course, includes an allowance for commission. You can make the same comparisons.

Frequently, owners develop an inflated idea of value — often because they have progressively added the price of any fittings they may have put aboard their sailboats over the years. But, in this regard, there is some similarity with cars: sticking a new engine into a ten-year-old banger may add a little to its worth, but nowhere near as much as the actual cost incurred. The exception would be the 'classic' whose value can be greatly increased if properly restored.

So, beware of wild pricing in private sales. An experienced yacht broker, because he knows he will have difficulty selling it, simply wouldn't list a boat that carried an outrageous price tag. You have no such assurance when dealing direct.

And expect to wear out some shoe leather. Whereas going through a broker can be 'one stop shopping', the road to buying privately can be littered with fruitless excursions and dashed hopes. I once drove to the East Coast, rowed across a creek in the pouring rain, and trudged at least a mile over muddy saltings to find that 'needs a little tidying up' actually meant it should be doused in petrol and torched.

Given mutual agreement on all points of the deal, there is absolutely no reason why private sales shouldn't proceed smoothly towards a satisfactory conclusion. But, unfortunately, some can degenerate into awful muddles. Recently I arrived to survey a yacht to find another surveyor already at work. The owner had actually sold the boat to two different people, taken deposits from both, and was stringing everyone along until he could see where the best possible advantage lay for himself. This is plainly an unacceptable way to conduct such proceedings. No one should be expected to pay for the cost of a survey without the clear understanding that, for the moment at least, he is the only one in the game. This sort of confusion would never arise if a competent yacht broker was overseeing the transaction.

So, having located your boat, and visited it to give it a provisional appraisal, what next? The saying that 'love is blind' is never more true than when someone is buying a boat. Perhaps the best advice would be to commit yourself to a compulsory cooling-off period of a day or so to think about it. After this, if your enthusiasm hasn't abated, you are obviously seriously infected and will be ready to move on.

First, go back and have another look at the boat. Try not to let eagerness get in the way of objectivity. Preferably, take along someone more experienced to act as Devil's Advocate, but (unless he's a professional) take even his opinion with a hefty pinch of salt. Look for serious structural defects, levels of maintenance and, as far as you can see, general deterioration in the material with which the boat is built. If possible examine the sails and other portable items very closely. These can represent a large proportion of the total value. If the equipment is worn out, the need for early replacement will add tremendously to the true cost of buying that particular vessel.

Having satisfied yourself that the boat is what you want, and that its condition is acceptable, the time has come to appoint a surveyor.

But first some money must change hands. If a yacht broker is handling the sale he will, on behalf of the vendor, require you to sign a **Sales Agreement** and pay a deposit (usually 10%) as an earnest of your intention to buy. Payment of the deposit effectively removes the boat from the market whilst negotiations between yourself and the owner are pending. It also protects the vendor against any damage that might be caused to his boat by yourself or your surveyor. If, in poking about, you leave the boat partially dismantled, the owner is within his rights to expect you to pay for its restoration.

The Sales Agreement is **subject to survey**, which protects you in two ways. If the surveyor's report reveals material defects not known or disclosed previously, you have the option either to negotiate the price lower, or to withdraw altogether from the deal. In the latter case, your deposit will be returned, less any costs which might have been incurred by the owner directly as a result of the survey. The 'subject to survey' clause is not, however, a loophole which allows you to renege frivolously. If you simply change your mind, or back out for trivial reasons, you could be on shaky ground when it comes to recovering your deposit.

In my opinion, the procedure should be much the same when buying privately. Agreements sealed with nothing more than a handshake are always friendly and convivial at the outset, but can become very contentious if the negotiations bog down. The best possible understanding is one where there can be no misunderstanding. Pay the owner a deposit (not necessarily 10% — a lesser amount will do) and exchange letters of agreement that the agreed price is subject to survey and that the deposit will be refunded if a significant problem arises. Better still use a standard agreement such as that issued by the **Royal Yachting Association.**

Generally, unless otherwise agreed, the buyer is responsible for any lift-out and scrub-off charges, as well as his surveyor's fee. Sometimes the owner will pay the yard bills himself. In this case, if the sale is completed, these costs will be added to the final payment. And, if the deal falls through, they will be deducted from the deposit before the balance is returned.

Surveys and Surveyors: Luckily for yacht surveyors, the custom of lopping off the heads of bearers of bad tidings has rather fallen into disuse — although I'm certain the temptation still lingers. For it often falls upon the surveyor's lot to inform some hapless yachtsman that the glorious swan of his dreams is actually a crippled goose.

The purposes of having a survey are fourfold: To protect a purchaser from investing in an outright wreck; to warn him of any aspects of the vessel's condition which could be a threat to his safety; to identify any defects and assess the costs of repair so that these can be considered in further negotiations on price; and to provide the kind of independent assessment of condition and value which may be required by an insurance or finance company.

The surveyor is paid by the purchaser and represents his interests. He is the counterpoise to the broker, who is working for the vendor. If a boat is over-priced a good surveyor will tell you so, and will suggest a more sensible figure. With regard to any defects which may have come to light in his inspection, he will confer with you about any ongoing negotiations you may wish to pursue, and will advise you if, in his view, you should withdraw altogether.

To some extent, survey reports are essays in pessimism, and can make gloomy reading. This is hardly surprising — indeed it would be worrying if this were not so. After all, your surveyor is employed to winkle out defects, not to eulogise glowingly on the more complimentary aspects of the yacht. However, most reports end with a summary which, if the surveyor has done his job properly, will set good against bad and give a balanced evaluation of the general quality and condition of the vessel. Experienced yacht owners, hardened to the depressive effects of surveys, usually read the last page first before embarking on the melancholy details buried in the text.

Most qualified surveyors belong to professional organisations which admit only people having suitable experience and technical credentials. The oldest of these is Britain's **Yacht Brokers, Designers, and Surveyors Association** — usually abbreviated to **YBDSA** — which was established in 1912. Members of the YBDSA all have many years experience and are carefully vetted by the Association before admission. They are obliged to comply with a strict Code of Practice and, as a condition of their membership, must also carry extensive Professional Indemnity Insurance to protect their clients against any losses resulting from possible errors or negligence. The Association, ever mindful of its reputation, is by no means slow to punish any professional malpractice that may occur. Expulsion from the organisation has been known.

If a surveyor doesn't belong to an accredited professional organisation, you have no means of knowing how competent he is or what degree of protection you will have if things go wrong. The man with the full beard, battered peaked cap, and foul smelling pipe, may look thoroughly nautical, but he could be (and often is) totally bogus. Check it out. And then hire a qualified professional.

And, should you have the boat surveyed at all? First, talk to your prospective insurers. If the boat is more than ten years old — younger for amateur built boats or unusual forms of construction — you will probably need a full condition survey for that purpose alone. If so, you might as well go ahead without further ado.

But what if the boat is only a couple of years old, and appears to you to be immaculate? Obviously, this is a matter of choice but my advice would still be a resounding YES! Newness is absolutely no guarantee that the boat is well found — indeed, I've conducted pre-commissioning surveys on brand new yachts and discovered some astonishing defects. Remember the well worn legal adage, *Caveat Emptor* — let the buyer beware. You may have legal recourse against a dealer if he sells you a

faulty boat out of his own stock 'in the course of his business', but private and brokerage sales are on an 'as is, where is' basis, and it's up to you to ensure that what you buy is in good shape. Whatever the age of the boat, the survey fee is likely to be only a small proportion of the total cost — an excellent investment in peace of mind.

Completing the Purchase: Once the boat has been surveyed, and a final price agreed, it's time to close the deal. Within the terms of the Sales Agreement, you will probably be required to come up with the balance of the cash within a fixed period — seven days is usual. But, before you part with this money, it's important to try to establish that the boat is actually the vendor's to sell!

Often this is a fairly straightforward matter. A continuous history of ownership may exist or the vessel may be Registered (more on this later) in a way which will show proof of ownership. But sometimes it can be less easy, and the purchaser should be wary.

A dentist acquaintance of mine once purchased a trim little wooden sloop laid up ashore in the boatyard where I have my office. He did a bit of work on it before launching it the following spring. But after a few month's use he decided it was not the boat for him and sold it on to a local school-teacher who set about some extensive renovation. During the course of this work a bookshelf was removed to reveal a series of letters and numbers carved into the fore-cabin bulkhead. The teacher knew instantly what these signified; they were the numerals required if a vessel is registered as a British Ship under Part 1 of the Merchant Shipping Act of 1894.

Curious to learn something of the history of his boat, the schoolteacher contacted the Registrar of Shipping, and was horrified when he was told that the boat had been reported stolen ten years previously and was, in fact, still the property of the Registered Owner at that time.

The upshot of all this was that the boat was returned to its rightful owner and the dentist was obliged to refund the full purchase price to the school-teacher. In turn, of course, the dentist could have sought redress from the man who had sold it to him but he, alas, had vanished without trace. And that man also could have been quite innocent, anyway, buying the boat in good faith as had the dentist. The chain of 'ownership' since the original theft could be very extended, and retracing it nearly impossible. Often it's the most recent parties who carry the can in these circumstances.

And sometimes a boat may be unofficially (and illegally) removed from

Registration to hide the fact that a lien exists against it — perhaps a loan from a bank or finance house or a judgement for some other debt. Another boat I had dealings with changed hands under an altered name and, when I looked into it, had apparently been sold two owners back long before an outstanding mortgage had been paid off. Presumably the then owner had received the cash for his boat and maintained the illusion of collateral so that he could continue to take advantage of the loan. In this case the loan had subsequently been cleared so the sale was able to proceed, but tidying up the procedural paperwork was an involved and fairly costly business.

It's also not possible to assume that because a yacht broker is handling the sale, he will be in a position to affirm that everything is squeaky clean. The broker simply takes the word of the vendor, who indemnifies him against any inaccuracies (whether intentional or not), by signifying his acceptance of the terms of the Brokerage Agreement.

So the moral is Be Careful! Examine the registration documents, or Bills of Sale or anything else that might help establish that the boat is being legitimately offered. If no other supporting evidence exists, you may need to make a decision based purely on your personal assessment of the status of the vendor. In this regard, it's reassuring to know that a man is well established in his job and home, and can be easily reached if anything goes wrong.

It always pays to use recognised forms of contract. The yacht broker will deal with these for you and will present you with all the correct paperwork on conclusion of the transaction. If dealing privately then acceptable contracts are obtainable (from the Royal Yachting Association, for example), or you may be able to get a copy of an appropriate Bill of Sale which you can duplicate and fill in yourself. At the very least, the vendor should confirm to you in writing that he has the right to transfer property in the yacht, and that it is 'free from all encumbrances, debts, liens and the like'. Registered (or, in the US 'Documented') vessels have their own forms and procedures, which must be used if title to the vessel is to be properly transferred. More of this in the next section.

Registration:

Over many centuries ships have provided the arteries for trade and expansion. Ships are large, mobile, and valuable objects whose use can have significant impact (sometimes literally) on the affairs of others. Both their commercial importance and their potential liability to third parties is immense, and it is therefore not at all surprising that it is internationally accepted that each ship should have a 'national identity' so that all can be identified and regulated.

Incidentally, the word 'ship' in legal terms doesn't necessarily mean some enormous behemoth with a cargo of containers or crude oil. Under British maritime law, for instance, a ship is described as any vessel 'used in navigation not propelled by oars'. Such a wide definition would embrace even outboard motor propelled inflatables and sailboards — and certainly every cruising sailboat. But this doesn't inevitably mean that the clammy hand of bureaucracy has got too tight a grip around the smaller boat — not yet, at least, and never if we stand our ground. Whereas merchant ships are obliged to comply with a number of complicated statutory requirements, at the other end of the scale the obligations relating to tiny dinghies are virtually none.

The precise methods of registration vary from country to country, but the British case is fairly typical and the broad procedures have been mirrored in certain other places — particularly by those nations where there are strong colonial links.

In Britain there are two possible forms of registration. The first is known as **Full Registration** which is covered by Part 1 of the Merchant Shipping Act of 1894 (from now on referred to simply as 'Part 1'). This is a fairly involved matter into which we shall delve more fully later in this section. Since the Merchant Shipping Act of 1983, however, there has been a simpler alternative to Part 1 registration: namely to enter a vessel on the **Small Ships Register** (commonly known as the **SSR**). The SSR is currently administered on behalf of the government by the Royal Yachting Association.

In Britain there is no statutory requirement for a yacht to be registered, provided it operates solely in UK waters. In some respects registration can be thought of in rather the same way as a passport — you don't need one if you stay at home but for travel abroad it's essential. But any yacht can be voluntarily registered, provided she is British owned, and there are usually advantages in this.

Small Ships Register:

As the simplest procedure, let's look at SSR first. It was brought into effect as a straightforward way for British sailors to acquire documentary evidence of the nationality of their vessels to satisfy foreign regulations.

An application form and guidance notes can be obtained from the RYA. This will require the owner to provide simple measurements and other details of the yacht. The fee for a five year registration is currently £10.00. If the vessel changes ownership before the expiry of this period, then the registration becomes renewable immediately.

For a yacht to be registered she must be:

- less than 24 metres (79 ft) long.
- owned by a Commonwealth or Irish Citizen resident in the UK. If two or more people own the vessel, then all must satisfy this condition.
- the vessel must not also be registered under the Merchant Shipping Act of 1894.

Convenient though SSR is, it also has its limitations. Briefly, these are:

- Marine mortgages cannot be recorded against this form of registry. If lenders require this form of security, then only Part 1 registry will be suitable.
- SSR does *not* provide proof of title. It is important to bear this in mind when buying a used boat.
- it is unsuitable for British citizens resident overseas. This would include extended cruises where the owner ceases to be resident (as a direct consequence of his cruise), and the yacht goes beyond the 5 year expiry period.
- the yacht cannot be registered in the name of a company or corporation.
- whilst generally accepted throughout Europe, some countries (the US, for instance) prefer visiting yachts to have Full Registry.

And remember that if you buy a second-hand boat already on the SSR, the existing registration becomes immediately void and you will need to re-register. This point is sometimes overlooked and can later land you in trouble in foreign ports. The French, for example, can get extremely awkward if the skipper's name is not the same as that shown on the yacht's papers. They may assume the boat to be illegally chartered (of which they take a very bleak view) or possibly even stolen. Either way, you can be guaranteed a rough passage.

Full (Part 1) Registration:

This is a much grander process which puts your yacht in the same legal bracket as the Queen Elizabeth. This is the only option available if:

- the yacht is over 24 metres in length.
- the vessel is owned by a company registered in the UK.
- any person or organisation lending money against the security of the vessel requires a mortgage to be registered against it.
- you are a British Citizen not resident in the UK.
- any part owner of the vessel, whether resident in the UK or not, is not a British Citizen.

The Registrar of British Shipping operates as a department of HM Customs and Excise. All the appropriate application forms and advisory notes can be obtained from their offices at any main Port of Registry.

For a new boat the process starts with the approval of your choice of name, which must be acceptable to the Registrar. This would exclude duplication of a name already on the registry, an offensive name, or one which could cause confusion in radio transmissions — *Mayday*, for example. The vessel must then be formally measured by an approved measurer or surveyor, and the paperwork processed to completion. Finally a **carving note** will be issued, which requires that the **official number** and **registered tonnage** be inscribed in accordance with certain requirements. Also, the name of the vessel and its Port of Registry must be painted conspicuously on the stern, again in the proper manner.

Amongst the other information you will need to produce will be a **Builder's Certificate** and, if you are not named on this, some documentary evidence (all documents of sale, for instance) which proves your ownership. Remember that Part 1 Registration provides proof of title, so it's important for the Registrar to establish without any doubt that the boat really does belong to you.

At current rates the various fees and other charges incurred in registering under Part 1 will cost you the best part of £400.

Registration of a second-hand boat can be accomplished in much the same manner, but it will be necessary to provide evidence that title passed correctly from owner to owner throughout the life of the vessel since new. This can be difficult, if not impossible, if the vessel is very old and past records are no longer available. However, the Registrar is empowered under the 1894 Act to take into account 'other adequate evidence', which would normally take the form of a statutory declaration of ownership and a sworn statement giving reasons why the other documentary evidence is missing. All of this adds to the costs, of course, and can be extremely aggravating. Faced with this, many yachtsmen opt for the less demanding requirements of SSR.

If buying a second-hand boat currently registered under Part 1, it's a fairly simple matter to have the registration transferred to your name. You must have paid for the boat, of course, and have the completed **Bill of Sale**, on which the transferor (seller) must be the same person or persons listed as the last owners on the **Official Registry**. This is an important but subtle distinction. the Certificate of British Registry, itself, is not proof of title as it could be subject to forgery. The only certain proof of title is the entry in the Official Registry, held by the **Registrar of British Ships** for the port in question.

Shares in a Part 1 Registered British Ship are divided into 64. Obviously, if a vessel is owned by a single person then he will own all of the shares. But if more than one person has a stake in the ownership then they can either own all of the shares jointly (in which case every share is owned collectively by the joint owners) or they can divide the shares between them in whatever proportions they choose.

Joint ownership is common amongst married couples where, if one were to die, his or her interest in the vessel would pass automatically (and irrespective of any will) to the other under the rules of survivorship. But this is unlikely to be an attractive arrangement amongst, say, friends, who would probably prefer to be part-owners, each with a distinct share in the vessel, disposable whenever or however he might wish.

Since the 1988 Merchant Shipping Act, the categories of persons qualified to own shares in a British Ship have been widened to include foreign nationals. However, this share must be a minority one (less than 32/64).

This recent concession solved something of a dilemma for Chele and me. Chele was born in Texas, and, although she has lived in the UK since 1979, proudly remains an American citizen. When Spook was built, and the matter of registration came up, we were faced with a problem. SSR was out of the question because all parties to ownership must qualify in terms of both residency and citizenship. Under Part 1, we were also unqualified for joint ownership of all 64 shares for the same reason. But (under Part 1 of the 1988 Act), Chele is entitled to own up to 31 shares of the boat in her own right. And that's the way we eventually arranged it — I own 33 shares in Spook and Chele owns 31. Not entirely fair, but the best we could do and be legal.

Interestingly, the reverse arrangement would not have been possible had we been living in the United States and wanted to 'document' Spook as a US vessel. The Americans remain chauvinistic about ownership and insist that all owners of the vessel be US citizens (though it is possible for non-citizens to have an interest in corporations or limited partnerships which, in turn, can own US vessels).

Documentation of US Vessel:

The procedure is very much the same as for a British vessel but is somewhat simpler and considerably cheaper (currently $100 compared to £370 — at today's exchange rates less than a sixth of the cost). Application forms and full procedural instructions are available from the Department of Transportation, US Coast Guard.

For a vessel to be eligible for documentation it must be over 5 nett tons and owned entirely by US citizens, a general partnership wholly owned by US citizens, a limited partnership at least 75% owned by US citizens, or by a US corporation complying to certain requirements.

Vessels of not more than 79 ft (24.08m) LOA, and barges and pleasure vessels (yachts) of any length used exclusively on the Great Lakes, can be measured by the owner or his agent using a simplified form of measurement. As in the UK, the application must be accompanied by a Builder's Certificate and conclusive proof of ownership (Bills of Sale).

There is no US equivalent of the British SSR scheme (which is nationwide), but most States have their own requirements for the registering and numbering of pleasure boats. Details of these can be obtained from the appropriate State authority.

FINANCE:

Apart from your house, a cruising sailboat is likely to be one of the most expensive items you'll ever buy. And, unless you're fortunate enough to be able to dip your hands into deeper than average pockets, it's also likely that you will be thinking of borrowing the money to pay for it.

Financiers are always eager to lend, but only at a price, and only if they can be pretty sure that you can repay the loan — with interest. Many different types of financial packages are available, and it's important to choose the one which suits you best in terms of both cost and convenience. It pays to shop around and — especially if there could be tax implications for you — it's often worth obtaining independent financial advice before you sign on the dotted line. Often, when examined closely, what would at first seem to be the best deal becomes less attractive when all the interacting factors are considered.

Marine Mortgages: Marine mortgages are loans secured by the vessel itself. As we've already discussed, in order for the mortgage to be recorded, a vessel must be registered under the Merchant Shipping Acts of 1894 and 1983 — though this is sometimes waived for smaller loans. The mortgage will be recorded by the Registrar of British Ships at the Port of Registry — though it won't appear on the Certificate of Registration. In the event of your bankruptcy or inability to keep up with the payments, the lender will have a prior claim to the vessel over other claimants.

Marine mortgages are perhaps the most popular form of yacht finance — especially for larger, more expensive vessels. The term of the loan is usually between 5 and 10 years, but can be extended to as much as 15 years in certain cases for large sums. The maximum advance is typically 80% of the purchase price (sometimes 75% for older vessels) and a survey and valuation may be required. There should be no penalties for early repayment of the loan.

Secured Loans: Similar to the marine mortgage but here the loan is secured against another asset — usually your house (where it becomes a mortgage on the property). This type of loan can often be repaid over a longer period than a marine mortgage — 20 years being not uncommon. But perhaps the most striking feature of such loans is that they can be raised for sums exceeding 100% of the purchase price — a powerful consideration if, say, you want to buy an old cheap boat and spend money on its restoration.

Interest rates vary, but are pretty much in line with marine mortgages.

Unsecured Loans: These are usually 'bank' loans lent against your personal credit-worthiness, with the maximum amount available being determined by how good a risk your bank believes you to be. However, although large sums are sometimes raised this way, unsecured loans are usually more suitable for smaller sums, borrowed over a fairly short repayment period. Interest rates vary considerably and, again, are influenced by your relationship with the bank. But, because the loan is unsecured and there is, therefore, an increased vulnerability for the lender, you can expect the rates to be at least a little higher than for a mortgage.

Interest-only loans: In this type of loan a capital sum is borrowed for an agreed period (usually short, say, less than five years), and monthly interest is paid on the total sum for that duration. None of the capital is repaid until the end of the term, when the loan terminates and the entire sum falls due.

This type of loan is attractive if you have expectations of a windfall — say a maturing endowment policy — and don't want to wait before buying your boat. However, for longer term loans a normal repayment loan is usually the better option as the interest tapers off as the capital is repaid.

INSURANCE:

Boats are mobile, valuable, and potentially dangerous projectiles which can both cause and suffer great damage if mishandled or adrift. They are also easy to steal, can sink if holed, and will burn merrily if ignited. Most yacht owners are therefore happy to allow their insurers to share in the risks.

At present, in the UK, there is no legal requirement to insure your boat, but if there is a marine mortgage or loan outstanding on it then the bank or finance company will probably insist that you do. Also, because of the possible risk to other boats and their crews, marina operators, and such people as river and harbour authorities, are very likely to require at least Third Party cover. Bearing in mind the very high awards for personal injuries that can be handed out by the courts these days, it seems only sensible anyway.

Marine insurance is a fiercely competitive business and rates vary from company to company. Factors which affect the degree of risk — and, as a consequence, the premium you will be asked to pay — include:

- The value of the vessel. In this regard it's important that this be quoted reasonably accurately when you fill out your proposal form. Insurers take a bleak view of boats being either grossly over or under valued. In the latter case, should it come to their notice in the event of a claim, they may pay only a proportion of that claim on the grounds that, hitherto, they have been receiving a smaller premium than the true value of the vessel should have yielded.
- The age of the boat. Boats are assumed to deteriorate with age. Many insurers require a full condition survey on boats over 10 years old, to reassure them that the vessel remains in good (and insurable) condition.
- Form of construction and materials used. The costs of repair vary with different methods. Traditional boats and those built with more exotic techniques call for special (and expensive) expertise. These extra costs obviously add to the risk and will be reflected in the premium. Many insurers won't have anything to do with ferro-concrete because of the difficulty in establishing how well the hull was built.
- Type of vessel. Again some insurers are wary of certain types. For example, multihulls have had a bad press over the years, and some insurers are unwilling to cover them.
- Your personal experience. Insurers are likely to charge higher premiums for beginners. Completion of recognised training courses (RYA, for example) will impress them and help reduce their rates. Some offer no-claims bonuses which, assuming you stay accident-free, will reduce premiums as experience grows.
- Cruising area. Obviously the more hazardous the voyage, the greater the risk to the vessel. Most policies place geographical limits on their cover — Brest to the Elbe, being common in UK waters — but this is rather dependant upon your experience. For instance, it would be relatively easy for an experienced yachtsman to get cover for a trans-ocean trip (at a price) but well nigh impossible for the novice. Many policies will require a minimum number of crew (usually three) for certain extended or risky passages, arguing that if one crew member

is incapacitated there will still remain sufficient aboard to bring the yacht back. For very small yachts, the insurers may limit usage to inshore and coastal waters — say, up to 12 miles offshore.

- Period afloat. In colder climates sailing is usually limited to the summer, whilst in the tropics it continues all year round. Quite clearly the risk is not the same for both cases and the insurers will adjust their rate accordingly. All too often — especially when there's an Indian summer — sailors are tempted to stay afloat beyond the limits of their policies, sometimes to be damaged in the autumn gales. Most insurance companies will cheerfully extend their cover (at additional cost) over a few extra weeks but it's important to arrange this in advance.

When you've arranged your insurance cover, be sure to read the small print so that you understand exactly what you're getting. Thankfully, these days the incomprehensible 'legalese' has given way to plainer words which should be pretty clear to all of us. Make sure that such portable items as outboards motors and dinghies are included in the cover — these are perhaps the easiest to lose or have stolen, after all. And think about your personal gear, and any cash or jewellery you may have aboard. When sailing abroad, arrange medical insurance to cover any treatment you may need. An acquaintance of mine recently had a wretched time in the West Indies after contracting hepatitis shortly after

Chapter 15
THE TRAINING

Until some years ago, it was generally accepted that the path to owning a cruising yacht almost always started with a small dinghy. This was certainly the case with me, and many others of my generation. Indeed, looking astern over the years, it seems that a considerable part of my youth was spent poking amongst the creeks and reed beds of the Hamble River or beating across the broader stretches of the Solent, perhaps to Cowes or Yarmouth. One learned by experience (often soggily gained) and the advice and criticism (often caustic) of those who had travelled the same route before. It was education by immersion and one learned, dare one say, almost by a process of osmosis.

Dinghies were our world. They were cheap and cheerful and could be abused awfully without complaint. Those gleaming yachts, moored out on the trots, were as far beyond us in terms of accessibility as the great Cunarders that then still plied the North Atlantic passenger trade.

But things are different today. The knockabout boats have almost disappeared. The scruffy mongrels of the sailing world are almost extinct. Nowadays youngsters are more inclined to go sailboarding which, although still dependant upon the basic principles of propulsion by the wind, isn't much help when it comes to learning the tricks of more conventional sailing. True, there are a number of dinghy classes still active, but these tend to be fragile, high performance craft; too twitchy, too unforgiving, and too darned expensive for latter-day Swallows and Amazons to muck about in. The present trend is for people to come directly into cruising. Their first boat is often of fair size, and usually bristling with the kind of gadgetry we have come to take for granted. This is, perhaps, a pity as it rather insulates the novice from the seat-of-the-pants sensations of sailing.

So, how do we go about learning the ropes? Sailing is a complex business with a diverse range of disciplines to master: Apart from the actual handling of his yacht — no mean art in itself — a cruising skipper must have a sound knowledge of navigation, meteorology, rules of the road, tidal calculations, radio procedures, ropework, and first aid. And then, of course, there's the preparation and maintenance. You can't just summon a mechanic if something breaks at sea. So, ideally, he should be a shipwright and engineer as well.

Crewing for someone else is a common introduction to sailing. And, if that person is competent and able to communicate his knowledge well, then much can be learned like this. If you are lucky enough to have such a friend, then your way is clear. At least the basic skills can be learned without major cost or commitment from yourself.

But others aren't so fortunate and are faced with either muddling through or seeking some structured form of tuition. Quite obviously the latter is preferable.

In Britain the Royal Yachting Association presides over a comprehensive range of educational programmes, covering levels of experience from the absolute novice to the ocean navigator. These take the form of shore-based courses — often held in the evening throughout the country as part of the Adult Educational programme — and practical courses (usually either of 5 day's duration or spread over three 2 day trips) actually aboard a suitable cruising boat under the supervision of a qualified instructor. All sailing schools (which may be an organisation or a single individual) are *vetted and approved by* RYA inspectors. Obviously the shore-based courses can only cover the theory, whilst those conducted at sea will also provide the hands-on experience you will need. A good plan is to enrol for both, wrestling with the theory ashore and consolidating it with hard-won experience afloat.

The practical, yacht-based courses usually end with an examination which, assuming you pass, entitles you to be issued with a **Certificate of Competence** for that particular grade. And it is *only* the practical course which lead to these certificates; the shore-based, theory courses earn Completion Certificates which, although certainly worthwhile, are not the same thing as those gained actually at sea. There are also minimum levels of sea-time required for each grade, much of which will be gained during the actual courses themselves.

Starting as a beginner, you would follow the series of courses in the following sequence:

Competent Crew — practical: A yacht-based course which assumes no previous knowledge or experience. Your instructor will help unravel the mysteries of sailing terminology and you will start to hone your skills at helmsmanship and boat handling. Basic seamanship will include sails, ropework, fire drill, safety, man overboard, weather, and the rules of the road. At its conclusion you will emerge equipped to be a useful crew member aboard a sailing yacht.

The RYA Certificate requirement is that you should have spent at least 5 days at sea, have sailed 100 miles, of which 4 hours must have been at night. This 'starter' course should cover this adequately.

Day Skipper — shore-based: For this some practical experience is desirable, but no other technical knowledge is assumed. Basic seamanship theory will be covered, and you will be introduced to navigation and meteorology.

Day Skipper — practical: A yacht-based course. Students should have gained a Competent Crew Certificate or have equivalent experience. This course builds upon subjects already covered, and gives emphasis to navigation and pilotage. Completion of this course will enable you to skipper a small yacht in familiar waters by day.

The RYA Certificate requires: 10 days. 200 miles. 8 night hours.

Coastal Skipper/Yachtmaster Offshore — shore-based: For those whose knowledge in navigation is already to a Day Skipper shore-based standard. This course rounds off the theoretical knowledge in navigation and pilotage required for offshore (but not ocean) cruising.

Coastal Skipper— practical: By now you will have been in charge of a sailing yacht in tidal waters, and will have made several passages by day and by night. This course concentrates on the responsibilities of skippering a boat: preparation for sea, passage planning, dealing with emergencies and adverse weather conditions, as well as extending your navigational abilities in the 'hands-on' situation.

RYA Certificate requirements: 20 days. 400 miles. 12 night hours.

Yachtmaster Offshore — practical: For many the final goal. This is usually a 7 day yacht-based course comprising 5 days of instruction followed by 2 days of examination. By this stage you will be a widely experience sailor with a good many miles under your belt. The course will round off your knowledge, reinforcing all that you have learned, and expanding still further your ability to command a yacht in almost any situation.

RYA Certificate requirements: 50 days. 2500 miles. At least 5 passages over 60 miles, including 2 overnight and 2 as skipper. In addition students must hold a Restricted VHF Licence and a First Aid Certificate.

Yachtmaster Ocean — shore-based: This is really a supplement to the Yachtmaster Offshore, adding celestial navigation, ocean meteorology, and long distance passage planning to the existing foundation of your skills.

RYA Certificate requirements: An ocean passage as skipper or mate of watch, for which evidence in the form of sights and other navigational records should be submitted.

British yachtsmen can count themselves fortunate to have these courses and qualifications at their disposal. And the Royal Yachting association should be heartily congratulated for their development and ongoing support. Some other countries — including Eire, Australia, and South Africa — have adopted them in their entirety; others have taken aboard parts of the programmes and modified them to suit their own purposes. An essential element in the scheme is that instruction be conducted in tidal waters, this obviously rules out the possibility of holding similar courses in such regions as the Mediterranean, the Caribbean, and parts of the United States, where tidal flows are too weak to be of much navigational consequence.

VHF Restricted Certificate of Competence: A VHF transceiver must only be operated by a person holding at least a Restricted Certificate of Competence or by a person operating under the supervision of a certificated operator. Obtaining a Certificate is a fairly straightforward matter, involving a few hours tuition and a simple test. The test covers the regulations and restrictions governing the use of VHF equipment, and, of course, operating procedures for normal and emergency traffic. Usually, both tuition and test are embedded within the RYA training scheme, but can also be taken separately at various centres around the country. In the USA the regulations are very similar, requiring VHF operators to hold at least a Restricted Radiotelephone Operator Permit. However, unlike the British certificate, this can be obtained without examination; the applicants simply declaring that they are familiar with the laws relating to radio transmissions, and that they can transmit spoken messages in the English language.

Sail Training Ships: From majestic square riggers to modern ocean-going yachts, almost every maritime nation has its collection of training ships. In Britain there are several, usually operated as charities or non-profit making trusts or companies. These exist under the umbrella of the **Association of Sea Training Organisations** — more commonly referred to as **ASTO**.

Obviously, even the smallest of sail training ships is likely to be a fairly complicated vessel when compared to a family yacht. It is therefore hardly surprising that all are commanded by qualified skippers and manned by a number of permanent crew members who will form the nucleus of the ship's company. But there are no *passengers* on a training ship. Everyone aboard — regardless of age or sex — is required to pull his weight.

Nearly all of these vessels concentrate on the training of youngsters — 12 to 25 years old being fairly typical limits. Some have a few berths for accompanying adults, and may even run special cruises entirely for adults on an occasional basis, but this is not usually their primary function.

And some ships draw at least a proportion of their crews from specific groups. For instance, the STS Lord Nelson, run by the Jubilee Sailing Trust, has been specially built to enable able-bodied and physically handicapped sailors to share the challenge of sailing a tall ship at sea; the TS Royalist — a 110 ton brig — draws its crews from the Sea Cadets and Boy Scouts; and the 72 ft (21.9m) Arethusa takes disadvantaged youngsters, often from inner city area, and introduces them to sailing in a series of 5 day cruises. More generally, the Ocean Youth Club has a fleet of nine 70 ft (21.3m) ketches, and a membership of over 4000 youngsters. The 138 ft (42.0m) brig Astrid makes regular transatlantic voyages from the U.K. to the West Indies. Details of these and other sail training ships are available from ASTO, c/o the RYA.

The Egremont provides unusual accommodation and a sailing base for the Island Cruising Club.

Of particular note for the prospective yachtsman is the **Island Cruising Club**, based in Salcombe, Devon, which was founded in 1951. Although constitutionally a limited company, in spirit the ICC is very much a club, run by dedicated staff members for the benefit of their fellows. After covering the overheads and other operating costs, all profits are ploughed back to improve the facilities and to add to the fleet.

The ICC has an office, club house and workshop facilities ashore. Moored out in the lovely estuary, just upstream of the town, is the steel ship, *Egremont*, which started life as a ferry carrying passengers across the River Mersey. She is now the ICC's sailing dinghy base, with accommodation for the club's staff plus berths for 55 members. The accommodation is by no means luxurious, but is entirely adequate and, many would say, appropriate to the nature of the club. The *Egremont* also provides an unusual social focus for cruising and dinghy members alike. The engine room, once vital when she was in commercial service, has long been stripped of its machinery and now enjoys an even more important function as the ship's bar.

The ICC membership numbers approximately 3,500 and spans all ages from 10 years old and upwards. These include many sailors from overseas, who come to Salcombe periodically, both to enjoy the excellent sailing and the quite unique *camaraderie* of the club. Beginners are welcome, and courses are available for their training, either on a fairly informal basis or to comply with the more structured requirements of the RYA scheme from Competent Crew to Yachtmaster Offshore. There are no complicated procedures for joining — no referees or stuffy selection committees. You simply pay a modest annual subscription to join and, thereafter, are charged on a varying scale for the use of the boats.

But perhaps the most exciting prospect offered by the ICC is the chance to sail a wide and unusual selection of boats without first becoming a millionaire. Apart from the stationary *Egremont* with its gaggle of sailboards, dinghies, and open keelboats, there is the cruising fleet which includes: *Hoshi,* a 72 ft (21.9m) gaff schooner, built in the Edwardian era as yacht; *Speedwell of Cremyll,* an elegant 49 ft (14.9m) yawl built in 1962; *Provident,* 70 ft (21.3m) of massively constructed Brixham sailing trawler dating from 1924; and a selection of smaller modern yachts. All of the cruising yachts carry experienced skippers (and mates on the largest boats) and are therefore available for members with any level of experience.

For many would-be sailors, teetering on the brink of committing themselves to positive involvement, it is difficult to conceive of an easier

Provident, *the Island Cruising Club's recently restored Brixham sailing trawler, lies at her mooring in Salcombe.*

or more economical entry into cruising than that offered by the Island Cruising Club.

Flotilla Holidays: Although not strictly intended for training purposes, these offer a marvellous opportunity for sailors to accumulate cruising experience and sea-time — often in some wonderfully exotic localities. The flotillas usually comprise a small fleet (of anything between eight and twelve yachts) which cruises loosely in company, under the watchful eye of a lead boat.

The lead boat carries the flotilla captain, who has overall responsibility for the fleet; an engineer, to take care of any maintenance that might be required; and a hostess to organise all those jollies ashore at day's end.

Most flotilla captains are young and enthusiastic. Despite their lack of years, they are chosen for their experience, which is often considerable. Although not professional instructors, they are understandably reluctant to see their boats abused, and are usually only too pleased to guide and advise. Acting as Mother Goose, they will watch closely over you (and the rest of their brood) as you all sail around the prescribed route. They will help you to get the best out of your boat, and will have a wary eye for any impending calamities. The lead boat maintains a continuous VHF radio watch, so is instantly contactable should a problem arise. Similarly, he can quickly advise you when he sees something going obviously wrong.

Quite understandably, the flotilla companies require their clients to have at least *some* experience before they will entrust their yachts to them. But these requirements aren't very demanding. Most grade the routes they use, and will encourage you to chose a relatively undemanding one if you are a beginner. Some companies organise familiarisation courses, which you can take ahead of time to prepare you for your vacation. This makes a great deal of sense if you are unsure of yourself, or moving to a type of boat with which you are unfamiliar.

The boats are invariably modern and are, of necessity, well-maintained. Crew sizes are usually between two to six people per boat, depending upon the number of berths available and how gregarious you wish to be. Obviously, the more people you have aboard, the more the cost is spread.

Flotilla holidays aren't cheap, but there are those who argue that, in cost terms, they make more sense than actually owning your own boat. After all, the argument goes, why have the hassle of all that maintenance when you can let someone else do it? And why restrict yourself to a single sailing area when you can enjoy so many? Flotilla holidays now operate in nearly all of the world's most seductive cruising waters — including the Mediterranean, the Caribbean, the Bahamas, and even in places as remote as the coast of Thailand. No doubt, within a few years, wherever you find clear waters and favourable weather conditions, there you will find a flotilla.

Crewed Charter: For those who prefer not to cruise in company with other boats, the charter yacht provides a useful, if more expensive, alternative. Some are unashamedly luxurious.

I recall an evening in the Caribbean, anchored in the wide sweep of Great Bay on the island of St. Martin. We had just taken a swim over the side and were sitting partially dressed on the coachroof, very refreshed, adding to our sensation of well-being by sampling a sundowner apiece. We had barely taken a sip when a magnificent staysail schooner came around the headland and dropped its hook not far distant. Uniformed crew members glided quietly about its deck. The sails furled as if by magic. An awning was unrolled and rigged between the masts. A table and chairs appeared. Candles were lit. Soft music and the gentle clink of ice-buckets could be heard.

Then, from somewhere below, there emerged a spectacular foursome; all tuxedos, shimmering gowns, and glinting jewellery. Fascinated, we watched as the flunkies converged and ushered them forward. Laughter floated across to us through the tropical air, and with it came the aroma of perfume and expensive cigar smoke. They took absolutely no notice of us, of course, though they could see our boat as plainly as we could theirs.

For such are the contrasts of sailing. And for the purpose of this book we can ignore the floating palaces with their large crews and fawning attendants. Certainly, their passengers have no interest in the sailing itself. The yacht becomes merely a vehicle to convey them from place to place in maximum comfort and luxury. And, whilst this is a perfectly legitimate pursuit, which I'm certain many of us would relish had we the chance, it obviously has nothing to do with learning to sail.

The type of charter yacht which would interest us is typically upwards of 40 ft (12m) long, and is crewed by two people, often husband and wife. Accommodation obviously varies with size but is always sufficient to take at least an average family group. As with flotilla holidays, the prime purpose is more recreational than instructional, but most skippers are willing to share their knowledge if you are eager to learn, and many make participation in the handling of the boat an important element in the kind of holidays they provide.

But check first. Some skippers prefer their charterers to be entirely docile. If you want to be a member of the crew and not just an item of baggage, then it's as well to make sure this is understood before you embark.

Crewed chartering gives you the opportunity to sail on yachts which are perhaps larger than you would at first wish to buy yourself. You will find the comparisons interesting. Contrary to common belief, large boats are in many ways easier to handle than small ones. Things happen slower and there is more room to organise the work. And neither are they so skittish under way. But the power in their sails is awesome, and this in itself is worth experiencing.

All in all, the gathering of expertise and experience should be a pleasurable process for you — not some dreadful rite of passage that has to be endured before you move on to better things. Taken a step at a time over a reasonable period, you will feel your enjoyment grow with understanding. And with increasing confidence will come relaxation. But it's important not to over-reach yourself. Better by far to cruise within your ability, extending your horizons as you progress, than to cast off into the wild blue yonder with nary a care.

As many have found to their cost, ignorance is almost *never* bliss at sea.

Chapter 16
THE SOCIAL LIFE

It was a late summer evening. The sun was nudging the hill-tops to the west, and the clouds were lurid with its light. A group of us were gathered on the yacht club verandah, glasses in hand. In the sort of mood that can be so easily induced by such surroundings, we were musing in a rather muddled way on the 'Delights of Cruising', as if it were some philosophical doctrine we were pursuing for vital but selfless reasons.

I seem to remember that I was for 'long voyages' and went on at some length about 'shaking off the fetters of the shore' and somesuch. Someone else babbled about 'new horizons' and 'different ports, different joys'. And a third discoursed on 'transcendentally discovering himself' and told us how he had been visited by Sir Francis Drake's mother whilst sailing single-handed to the Azores, and had subsequently become convinced that he was the reincarnation of that piratical Elizabethan.

Amidst these maunderings, one of our number remained virtually silent. Lounging back in his chair, he listened to the conversation, offering only the occasional smile or nod. Much later, with the moon now fully risen and the Bar Steward growing restless to go home, our friend made his only contribution. Putting down his drink, he linked his fingers over his belly and spoke. 'What I like best of all about sailing', he said, 'is to leave the bloody boat safe in its berth, and to come down here and talk about it.'

This, as we all agreed, was a man who knew a thing or two about life.

There are few places as empty as the open sea, and few more crowded than the average marina. Cruising has much to do with contrasts, and nowhere is this more evident than in the extremes between solitude and sociability. Perhaps this is one of its main attractions. There is no doubt that to 'get-away-from-it-all' offers a useful catharsis, but to return at the end of a trip and to share one's reminiscences with fellow sailors is, for most of us, a great part of the pleasure.

Many of these encounters occur spontaneously. A chance meeting with a boat you know, or a hail from a stranger to row over and join another crew, have resulted in some memorable exchanges. I've spent countless hours in the cockpits of other people's yachts, yarning into the small hours, often over fairly generous draughts of the local hooch.

And these occasions have more than a purely social value. Apart from

Marinas can be crowded places. St. Peter Port, Guernsey in high summer.

An international fleet assembles at a classic boat rally in Palma de Mallorca.

the yachting gossip that we all enjoy, an amazing amount of useful information can be garnered. Careful passage plans suddenly unravel in the light of 'There's this wonderful little restaurant in...' or 'Oh, boy, did we drag our anchor in...'

All recreational pursuits have their grapevines. The cruising one is particularly vigorous and, especially for the novice, is a priceless well of accumulated experience from which to draw.

Yacht Clubs: Where two or more enthusiasts are gathered together, there they will form a club. This is a basic law of life and, despite the fact that their activity takes them away from land (which would seem to defeat the object), yachtsmen tend to conform to it.

Yacht clubs vary enormously in the degrees of swankiness to which they aspire. The grandest can be like marbled palaces, roamed by obliging flunkies ready to fulfil your slightest whim. On the homelier side can be found rickety shacks, clinging to muddy creek banks, where the members take turns to tend the bar or mend the roof. Some are yacht clubs in name only, with the emphasis heavily on the social life. Once at a 'Club Nautico' in Vigo, Spain, I was wandering around, towel in hand, looking for the shower when I burst through a door to find myself in the middle of a harp recital. Others resemble country clubs, with tennis courts, swimming pools, or even golf courses attached. Between these varying extremes lie every shade of pomp and grandeur.

The costs of membership are almost directly proportional to the popularity of the club and the levels of luxury and other services provided. Market forces prevail. Some of the posher clubs are very expensive whilst others of more modest pretensions are usually much more reasonable.

And so it is with exclusivity. Membership of some clubs — whether because of social *cachet* or the splendid facilities they offer — can involve an extended period on a waiting list. One club I heard about is rumoured to have a waiting list for the waiting list. Others may require a particular qualification (applicants to the Royal Ocean Racing Club, for example, must have competed in a Fastnet Race). Some are strictly by invitation only.

But, happily, by far the majority of yacht clubs are both approachable and affordable. There will probably be one in your chosen sailing patch which will suit both your pocket and your social preferences. Inquiries amongst other yachtsmen in the region will give you a good idea of the flavour of each club, and there is no reason why you shouldn't visit and talk to the Secretary and other members, who will be pleased to discuss such details as conditions of entry, the various activities of the club, and the costs involved.

Joining a club typically involves providing at least two referees who must be current members in good standing. Applicants are usually then interviewed by a selection committee who will give them the once-over and decide whether or not they are suitable persons to be welcomed to the fold. This, of course, is a two-way encounter which also gives the applicant an opportunity to question the committee and to establish if they're the sort of people he would like to rub shoulders with. After acceptance, some clubs insist on a probationary period for new members (usually somewhat coyly called Associate Membership) after which they are taken aboard on a permanent basis.

Whereas some yacht clubs are rather specialised — the Ocean Cruising Club, for instance — others operate on a broader sailing front. My own club is a good example. Somewhat middle-of-the-road in terms of cost and plushness, it is involved in ocean racing, local round-the-buoy racing, twelve different classes of dinghies, and a local one-design keelboat which is hotly competed. There are also less formal races for the large cruiser fleet (some of which are organised specifically for man and wife crews) and joint cruises to a variety of destinations along the English and French coasts. A cadet section encourages the youngsters and brings them forward until, one day, they will move on to more ambitious things. All this plus a good restaurant and an enthusiastically patronised bar makes for a rich and varied sailing mix.

Not all yacht clubs are swanky places. Redclyffe Yacht Club clings to the banks of the River Frome at Wareham.

One of the most significant advantages in belonging to a yacht club is the reciprocal hospitality extended by many other clubs when you are sailing outside your home waters. To be able to meet other sailors and to take advantage of local knowledge — let alone the showers and other facilities — is a great boon when you are far from home. But tread carefully. Not all clubs are hospitable, and some are downright frosty. Remember, especially when abroad, that a few are actually social clubs in disguise; and to arrive in your salt-rimed sailing gear to mingle with the minks and pearls is to be very much a fish out of water. And the kind of clubs preoccupied with racing are unlikely to smile too kindly upon a casual cruising yachtsman.

Don't take acceptance for granted. You can't just wander in, plant your stern on a bar stool, and call for a beer. If you get the chance, inquire ahead. Write or telephone to clubs along your route to see if you would be welcome. If this isn't practicable, make contact on VHF immediately before you arrive, or call on the Secretary or Boatman when you get ashore. Some clubs commendably take a very positive interest in visiting yachts — rightly believing that they enrich and enliven their own activities. Some even have visitors' moorings which you can use for a few days — usually at low cost and, sometimes, free.

And, when you have been welcomed, treat the host club with respect. Honour their dress codes and other protocols and, perhaps, return their hospitality by entertaining a few members aboard your own boat. Pay any bills or temporary membership dues without complaint. Whether they are your kind of folk or not, you will find them the way they like it, and it's their backyard after all.

Sailing Associations: Although the distinction sometimes gets blurred, perhaps the main difference between yacht clubs and sailing associations lies in the diffuse nature of the latter. Whereas the activities of a club are centred around the club house, sailing associations tend to be organisations whose purpose is to promote (and sometimes regulate) the common interests of its members.

In Great Britain the **Royal Yachting Association** sits like a mother hen over the whole sailing scene, co-ordinating all aspects of boating. It administers the racing, acts as an advisory body to the government, represents the country within the **International Yacht Racing Union**, and monitors and acts as a pressure group wherever the interests of yachtsmen are affected or threatened. Additionally, the RYA has been responsible for developing the excellent series of training programmes leading to the various certificates of competence that sailors can attain.

Other services include specialised legal advice, and a selection of informative booklets on a host of different topics.

Much of the RYA's work goes unseen, but is of immense value to the whole boating community. Acting as a powerful counterpoise to the encroachments of bureaucracy, the Association has done sterling work resisting the imposition of nonsensical regulations, whilst still encouraging developments which make our sport safer and more pleasurable.

The costs of personal membership are low, and the benefits of being a member considerable. Although the functions and activities of the RYA are primarily of interest to British sailors, those in other countries would also be welcomed aboard. Yachting is an international activity, with considerable cross fertilisation of ideas based on common interests. The more we know about each other, the better it is for all of us.

Other countries have their own boating organisations, but none enjoy quite the position of the RYA. The Boat Owners Association of the United States offers technical assistance to American sailors and is also active in legislative and conservation programmes relating to boating. The National Boating Federation is a federation of national, state, and regional boating organisations, yacht clubs and individuals, which keeps members informed on legislative developments, and provides an elected voice for the American boating public.

In various parts of the world, wherever they are popular, other associations cover the activities of a single class of vessel, or perhaps different classes made by the same boatbuilder. These groups often have a strong social content, organising races, rallies and other gatherings, depending upon their preferences. For cruising sailors, more used to journeying alone, these get-togethers can be immensely enjoyable and the chance to compare performance boat-for-boat offers a rare chance to hone one's sailing skills under the pressure of some mildish competition.

Many associations distribute newsletters to keep owners abreast of the movements of boats and as a forum in which to discuss any other matters which might be of interest. The Cruising Association, based in London, is particularly ambitious, publishing a 'Handbook' (really a very comprehensive cruising guide) based on navigational information gathered by its members. This guide runs to over 500 pages and covers British waters and the European coast from the southwest Baltic to the Straits of Gibraltar.

Sailors tend to be a friendly bunch, given to displays of extrovertness they would be embarrassed to show ashore. To wave merrily at every car you pass would soon have you hauled off to the funny farm, but these informal salutes are almost obligatory between passing yachts. Of course there are those whose attitude is too incurably jaundiced to ever crack a smile, but these are only the most hardened cases. Perhaps as a compensation for the isolation of being at sea, sailors relish these personal contacts and, indeed, will often alter course to make some sort of chummy exchange possible.

This agreeable human phenomena brings its responsibilities. The sea is quite harsh enough without having to suffer the oafishness of others, and it's up to all of us to preserve harmony as best we can. As a commodity, courtesy is free and we can all afford to splash it around a bit.

Respect privacy. Give other boats at anchor as wide a berth as necessary - certainly enough to swing when the tide or wind turns.

Try to tread carefully over other boats when rafted up alongside. Others may be asleep below and, even if not, probably don't want to experience your impersonation of an elephantine clog dancer on their deck above. And please don't share your choice of music or line in jokes with everyone else when you finally get back to your boat. Boats are thin-walled capsules, usually with poor acoustic insulation, and sound carries very well over water.

Take your garbage home with you — at least the items the fish won't eat. Despite its immensity, the sea can't cope indefinitely with the refuse that's dumped into it. We have a collective responsibility not to add to its pollution and, as sailors, a personal interest in keeping it clean. Plastic bags foul propellers and clog engine cooling water intakes — not to mention the damage they do to marine and bird life. Larger jetsam can be especially menacing. In 1971, a boat I designed was in a collision with a galvanised steel water tank, floating in the Thames Estuary. The crew were taken off by the Brightlingsea lifeboat, slightly frostbitten but thankful not to lose their lives.

And be mindful of local customs and sensibilities. It doesn't take much imagination to appreciate how accepted standards of decorum can vary. Nude or topless sunbathing may be perfectly acceptable in liberally minded places, but can be deeply shocking in regions where even skimpy clothing — let alone nakedness — is considered offensive. Some years ago, whilst walking through a small southern Italian village, I was berated by an elderly lady for merely walking hand in hand with a girlfriend. Unwittingly we had caused offence, and had rightly been taken to task for our clumsiness.

Flag etiquette is another area which can either compliment or offend, and a few words on this may be in order. Customarily, a yacht flies its maritime ensign from its stern, either on a pole, from a halyard bent some way up the backstay, or sometimes from the mizzen head if a ketch or yawl. In Great Britain, this would most usually be the Red Ensign (never the Union Jack) or, subject to special permission and conditions, the white ensign (Royal Yacht Squadron only) or blue ensign, which can either be plain or **defaced** — i.e. with a club emblem. Other nations have their own national ensigns which are flown in similar fashion.

Any ensign should only be flown *during the hours of daylight*, and should be lowered at sunset or at 2100 hours, whichever comes sooner. Although many yachtsmen are rather sloppy about this, and are inclined to leave their ensigns up from one end of the season to the other, the owner of a well run yacht will take pride in his compliance with long standing tradition. Some yacht clubs can be decidedly sniffy about flag drill. I recall a hair-raising drive through Norfolk, Virginia. The owner of a boat I had designed had dressed it overall in honour of my arrival and, after meeting my delayed flight at the airport, was now desperately trying to get to his club before sunset to take all the flags down again. Apparently he would have been carpeted by the commodore for a single lapse, and could even have faced suspension had he repeated the offence!

When overseas the maritime ensign of the host country should be flown from the starboard crosstree. This is termed a **courtesy flag**, which defines its purpose very aptly. A brief tale illustrates its importance.

In 1974 on a transatlantic trip, I decided on a change of plan and put into Madeira rather than my intended port of call in the Canary Islands. We anchored in Funchal harbour. Now, Madeira is Portugese territory and, because we hadn't expected to be there, we weren't carrying the correct courtesy flag. At the sight of our naked crosstree, the boarding Customs Officer became thoroughly affronted and, despite our explanation and our promises to put the matter right without delay, gave us a pretty hard time before he stamped our papers.

Unfortunately, when we got ashore we found Funchal in turmoil. A bloodless coup had been mounted throughout Portugal to depose the dictator, Salazar. The town was swarming with military vehicles and personnel. The populace, in an outpouring of patriotism and sheer delight at the fall of the tyrant, appeared to have invested heavily in their national flag. There was not one to be had in any of the shops.

Eventually, after some cajoling and an exchange of hard cash, we bought a large and somewhat tattered Portugese flag from the owner of a waterfront restaurant.

What happened to us next was rather unexpected. Within minutes of our hoisting our newly acquired 'courtesy ensign', the customs launch was alongside again and our now even less friendly officer was complaining thunderously that we were making a mockery of himself and his country by flying such a shabby and grotesquely huge flag. For some minutes he raged up and down the decks, threatening all manner of retribution against the arrogant British with their misplaced post-imperial sarcasms. It took some delicate diplomacy and the best part of a bottle of whisky to calm things down. We eventually parted cordially enough, but the incident left an indelible impression on me. Courtesy flags, properly flown, are a visible acknowledgement of the respect we should bear other countries. To be careless about such things is to invite the justifiable wrath of people who might otherwise be our friends.

If you are a member of a club or association then a distinguishing burgee (a small triangular flag) can be flown. Properly, the burgee should be carried at the masthead but, with the profusion of antennae, wind sensors, and other paraphernalia up there, this is often impracticable. These days it is not uncommon to see a club burgee flying from the starboard crosstree, but, if a courtesy ensign is also flown, then the latter should enjoy the superior position. As with all other flags, the burgee should be lowered at night, but, perhaps even more so than with ensigns, the trend is to leave them flying so long as the owner is aboard. Incidentally, the burgee indicates that the owner or person in charge of the yacht is a member of that club — not the yacht itself.

Flags are not expensive items, and should be replaced before they become old and frayed. An ensign which looks as if it went through the Battle of Jutland can make even the smartest yacht look untidy.

As with most pursuits, sailing has its own special protocols and social rules. Some of them are splendid, some are silly, and some are quite splendidly silly. But it is all part of the rich ferment and to be involved can be extremely fulfilling.

Cruising under sail is not just about techniques. It's about meeting other people in extraordinary circumstances, and mixing with them in ways often stifled by restrictive manners ashore. Welcome aboard.

GLOSSARY:

Listed below are only a few of the more commonly used terms which form the rich vocabulary of the sea. There is some duplication of definitions already given in previous pages, which I have covered again to provide a more accessible reference. And some of the definitions are so basic as to be almost insulting — for which I apologise.

It's never easy to define technical terms without using other jargon which may be equally baffling. Where I have done this the words are italicised and their definitions can be found elsewhere in the glossary.

Aback: A sail is said to be aback when the wind strikes it on its *lee* side.

Abaft: Further towards the *stern.*

Abeam: At right angles to the boat's centre-line.

Aft: At the *stern.*

Akas: The cross-beams joining the hulls of a trimaran.

Amas: The outer hulls of a *trimaran.*

Amidships: The centre of the boat, longitudinally and laterally.

Anemometer: An instrument for measuring wind speed.

Antifouling: A toxic paint applied to the underwater areas of the hull to inhibit 'fouling' (the accumulation of marine growths).

Apparent wind: The direction and speed of the wind as experienced by an observer on the boat. It is a combination of the *true wind* and the forward movement of the boat.

Astern: Behind the boat. To put the engine astern means into reverse.

Athwarthships: Across the boat from side to side.

Back: (1) When the wind backs, its direction changes anti-clockwise

(2) To 'back a sail' means to sheet it in such a manner that the wind fills it on the side which is normally to *leeward.*

Backstay: Part of the *standing rigging.* The stay which runs from the top of the mast to the stern, resisting the forward pull of the sails.

Baggywrinkle: A furry covering to parts of *standing rigging* which could chafe the sails.

Ballast: Extra weight placed low down on a boat to provide stability. It can be in the form of a ballast keel (usually of lead or iron), bolted below the boat or encapsulated within the hull, or loose in the form of ingots or other heavy objects.

Batten: A flexible strip fitted into pockets on the *roach* of a sail to assist it maintaining its shape.

Beam: (1) The maximum breadth of the boat.
(2) A transverse structural member supporting the deck.
(3) 'On the beam' means in a direction at right angles to the boat's centre-line.

Beam reach: The *point of sailing* where the wind blows in from approximately *abeam.*

Bear away: To steer the boat away from the wind.

Bearing: The direction of an object from an observer, usually expressed in compass degrees, either true or magnetic.

Beat: To sail a zig-zag course as close towards the wind as practicable. To be *close-hauled* on alternate *tacks.*

Bend: (1) To lash a sail to a *spar.*
(2) To knot two lengths of rope together - a bend is a knot used for this purpose.

Berth: (1) To moor a boat in harbour, and the space it occupies.
(2) A bed aboard a boat.

Bight: A loop of rope.

Bilge: The lower part of a hull.

Bilge keels: Twin plates or *keels* which protrude from the hull *outboard* of the centre-line.

Bilge-keeler: A boat fitted with *bilge keels.*

Bilge-water: Water which collects in the *bilge.*

Bimini: A *cockpit* sun awning rigged on a metal frame, which can be hinged down when not in use.

Block: A pulley made up of a *sheave* (or *sheaves*) in a wood, metal, or plastic body around which a rope runs.

Boom: The horizontal *spar* to which the *foot* of a sail is secured.

Bottlescrew: See **Rigging screw.**

Bow: The front end of the boat.

Bowsprit: The fixed *spar* protruding forward of the *bow* of a boat.

Broad reach: The *point of sailing* between a *beam reach* and a *run,* with the wind blowing over the *quarter.*

Bulkhead: A partition or 'wall' in a boat, usually fitted *athwartships.*

Bumpers: American term for *fenders.*

Burgee: A small triangular flag signifying membership of a yacht club or association.

Carvel: Wooden planking which is fitted edge-to-edge, giving a smooth external surface.

Catamaran: A *multihull* boat with two hulls of equal size.

Catboat: Properly a boat with a single sail, but the term has been expanded ('cat-rigged') to include boats with more than one mast where each mast only carries a single sail.

Caulking: The material — usually cotton, oakum, or a mastic compound — 'caulked' into the seams between planks to make them watertight.

Centreboard: A board lowered through a slot in the hull to help resist *leeway.*

Chain plate: A metal plate or bracket bolted to the hull or deck of a boat to which the *shrouds* or *backstays* are attached.

Chart: A nautical map providing navigational information for the area covered.

Chine: Usually seen on boats built from flat sheets (often steel or plywood). It is the line formed by the junction of the *topside* panels with those forming the bottom of the hull.

Cleat: A deck fitting around which ropes are wound in figure-of-eight fashion to secure them.

Clevis pin: A pin which closes the forks in certain end fittings to secure them. A typical application would be at the lower ends of *rigging screws.*

Clew: The aft lower corner of a sail, where the *foot* and *leech* meet.

Clinker: A method of construction in which adjacent planks overlap, producing a 'stepped' external surface. Known as lapstrake in the US.

Close-hauled: The *point of sailing* with the wind as close to the *bow* as practicable.

Close reach: The *point of sailing* between *close-hauled* and *beam reach,* with the wind blowing from forward of the *beam.*

Close-winded: This describes a boat which can sail exceptionally close to the wind.

Coamings: The raised barriers around the *cockpit* and *hatches* which help keep the water at bay.

Cockpit: The area on deck from which a boat is controlled. Cockpits are usually protected by coamings, dodgers, and spray hoods to increase crew comfort and safety.

Cotter pin: See **Split pin.**

Course: The direction in which a vessel is steered.

Courtesy ensign: The national flag of the host country flown by a visiting yacht as a mark of respect.

Cringle: An eye in a sail, traditionally formed by a small loop of rope, but these days more often a metal or plastic fitting.

Dead run: A *point of sailing* with the wind blowing from directly *astern.*

Deviation: A compass error caused by metal objects on the boat. Expressed in degrees, deviation is the difference between the direction indicated by a compass and the magnetic direction that should be indicated.

Displacement: The weight of water displaced by a boat afloat.

Dodgers: Canvas screens rigged on the *lifelines* to give additional protection to the crew in the *cockpit.*

Downhaul: Part of the *running rigging.* A rope which pulls down a sail or *spar.*

Draught: Draft in the US. The vertical distance between the *waterline* and the lowest point of the boat when afloat.

Drop keel: A *ballasted keel* which can be raised and lowered, somewhat in the manner of a *centreboard.*

Echo-sounder: An instrument for measuring the depth of water.

Ensign: A distinguishing maritime national flag.

EPIRB: An emergency radio distress beacon. The name is an acronym for Emergency Position Indicating Radio Beacon.

Fairlead: A deck fitting though which ropes (often mooring lines) are run, to alter the direction of the 'lead' whilst minimising chafe.

Fathom: A measurement (with metrication, now increasingly less used) for indicating the depth of water. 1 fathom = 6 feet (1.83m).

Fiddle: A raised lip fitted around the edge of tables, to prevent objects sliding off when the boat *heels.*

Foot: (1) The bottom edge of a sail.
(2) The bottom end of a mast.

Forestay: Part of the *standing rigging*. The foremost *stay* leading forward from the mast to the boat's *bow,* on which the *headsails* are usually *hanked.*

Freeboard: Vertical distance between the *waterline* and the top of the deck.

FRP: In the US, short for Fibreglass Reinforced Plastic.

Gaff: The spar to which the *head* of a quadrilateral sail is *bent.*

Galley: A boat's cooking area - kitchen.

Gelcoat: The outer coating (often pigmented) of a GRP moulding.

Genoa: A large *headsail* which overlaps the *mainsail.* Genoas are used in light to moderate weather conditions.

Gimbals: An arrangement of two concentric rings, pivoted at right angles, in which suspended objects remain level regardless of the *heel* of the boat. Cookers are often referred to as being gimbaled, which is actually incorrect as they swing only about a single axis.

Go about: To change *tack.*

Gooseneck: The articulated joint between mast and *boom.*

Goosewing: To sail downwind with the *headsail* sheeted on the opposite side as the *mainsail.*

Ground tackle: Anchoring equipment.

GRP: Glass Reinforced Plastic — fibreglass.

Guardwires: See Lifelines.

Gudgeon: See Pintle.

Gybe: To change *tack* by turning the boat's *stern* through the wind. Sometimes spelled *Jibe.*

Halyard: Part of the *running rigging.* Rope or wire used to hoist sails.

Hank: A specialised clip used to secure the *luff* of a sail to a *stay.*

Head: (1) The top corner of a triangular sail.
(2) The upper edge of a quadrilateral sail.

Hatch: An opening in the deck providing access to the interior of the boat.

Heads: Toilet. Actually, more correctly 'head', though heads has become common usage.

Headsail: Any triangular sail set forward of the mast.

Headway: The forward movement of a boat.
Head-to-wind: When the boat's *bow* is pointing directly into the wind.
Heave-to: To sail with the *headsail aback* and the *tiller* lashed to *leeward.* Most boats will lie quietly with the sails trimmed thus, making little headway.
Heel: Leaning to one side.
Inboard: Towards the centre-line of the boat.
Jackstays: Lines running along the deck to which safety harnesses can be clipped.
Jib: A small *headsail.*
Jibe: See *Gybe.*
Kedge: A second anchor, smaller than the primary **(bower)** anchor.
Keel: The backbone of a traditional boat. These days also a *ballast keel* bolted to the bottom of a boat.
Ketch: A two-masted rig with the *mizzen* shorter than the main mast.
Lapstrake: See *Clinker.*
Lateen: A triangular sail set on a pivoting *spar,* common on boats of the Middle East and Indian Ocean.
Lee cloths: Canvas restraints which can be rigged to prevent a person rolling out of a bunk when the boat *heels.*
Lee helm: The tendency for a boat to *bear away* from the wind.
Lee shore: Any shore onto which the wind is blowing.
Leech (1) The aftmost edge of a triangular sail.
(2) Both sides of a square sail.
Leeward: Away from the wind. The leeward side of a boat is that opposite to the one exposed to the wind. Opposite of *windward.*
Leeway: The movement of a boat downwind of its intended *course* due to the sideways pressure of the wind.
Luff: The forward edge of a sail. To 'luff up' is to turn the boat *head-to-wind.*
Mainsail: The fore-and-aft sail hoisted up the *aft* side of the main mast.
Mizzen: The fore-and-aft sail set on the *aft* mast of a *ketch* or *yawl.*
Outboard: (1) Away from the centre-line of the boat.
(2) Short for 'outboard motor'.
Painter: The bow line with which a dinghy is secured.

Pintle: A rudder fitting with a pin which, combined with a *gudgeon,* forms the pivot around which a rudder swings.

Pitch: (1) The angle of attack of propeller blades.
(2) The fore and aft plunging motion of a boat in heavy seas.

Point of sailing: The boat's *course* in relation to the wind direction.

Port: The left hand side of a boat, looking forward. Opposite to *starboard.*

Port tack: A boat is said to be on port tack when the wind strikes the *mainsail* on the port side.

Proa: A *multihull* boat having two hulls of different size, with the mast stepped on the larger hull. The proa *goes about* by changing direction end-for-end in a form of *gybe,* where the *bow* becomes the *stern* and vice-versa.

Pulpit: A metal guard rail fitted to the *bow* for crew security.

Pushpit: Similar to the *pulpit* but fitted to the *stern.*

Quarter: Midway between *astern* and *abeam.* 'On the quarter' means about 45° *abaft* the *beam.* 'Quartering seas' means waves that strike a boat on its quarter.

Rake: The angle at which a mast, or any other part of the boat, deviates from the perpendicular.

Rating: A handicapping system based on measurements and a complicated formula, which allows different sizes of boat to race against one another.

Reach: A *point of sailing* with the wind on or near the *beam.*

Reef: To reduce the area of a sail by folding or rolling.

Rigging screw: A screw device for tightening the *standing rigging.* Also known as a *bottlescrew* (UK) and a *turnbuckle* (US).

Roach: The curved part of the *leech* of a sail.

Run: A *point of sailing* with the wind blowing from *astern* or thereabouts.

Running rigging: All ropes such as *sheets* or used to handle and control the sails.

Scantlings: The measured size of structural components used in boatbuilding.

Schooner: A boat with two or more masts where the masts are either of equal height or the aftmost are taller than the foremast.

Scope: The length of anchor chain or rope paid out when anchoring.

Scuppers: Holes or gaps in the toerail which allow water to drain from the deck.

Sea room: Amount of sea area available for a boat to manoeuvre between itself and the land or other dangers.

Seacock: A shut-off valve on any underwater inlet or outlet passing through the hull.

Set: (1) The direction of *tide* or other current.
(2) To hoist a sail.
(3) The shape of a sail when drawing.

Shackle: A D-shaped metal link with a removable pin across the open mouth, used to connect things together.

Sheave: A grooved rotating wheel in a *block* or *spar* for a rope or wire to run on.

Sheet: Part of the *running rigging*. The rope attached to the *clew* of a sail which allows it to be correctly trimmed or 'sheeted'.

Shrouds: Part of the *standing rigging*. The wires which provide the sideways support for the mast.

Sloop: A single-masted boat with a *mainsail* and one *headsail.*

Sole: What would be called a 'floor' ashore. The walkways in the cabin and *cockpit.*

Spar: A general term describing any of the 'poles' (*mast, boom, gaff,* etc.) used to set or control the sails.

Spinnaker: A large lightweight ballooning sail used mainly when *running* but also (with certain types of spinnaker) when *reaching.*

Splice: A method of forming eyes in ropes or joining them together by interweaving their separate strands.

Split pin: A divided pin which, by opening the ends and turning them back on themselves, various fittings (especially clevis pins) are secured. Called *cotter pins* in the US.

Spray hood: A folding canvas shelter which can be rigged over a *hatch* to help keep the water out.

Spreaders: Horizontal struts projecting from the side of masts, allowing the *shrouds* to provide more effective support.

SSR: Small Ships Registry - administered by the Royal Yachting Association.

Stanchions: Upright metal posts supporting the *lifelines*.
Standing rigging: The *shrouds* and *stays* which support the masts.
Starboard: The right hand side of the boat, looking forward. Opposite to *port*.
Starboard tack: Sailing with the wind striking the *mainsail* on the *starboard* side.
Stay: Any wire forming part of the *standing rigging* which supports the mast in a fore and aft direction.
Staysail: Any sail which is *hanked* to a *stay*.
Stem: The piece of timber forming the *bow* of the boat, on which the planking terminates, or the equivalent area in a non-timber boat.
Stern: The rear of the boat.
Stiff: A boat is said to be stiff when it is especially resistant to *heeling*.
Tack: (1) The lower forward corner of a sail. 2) To *go about* through the wind so that the sails are filled from the other side.
Tacking: Making successive *tacks*. The boat will follow a zig-zag *course*.
Tang: The metal plates on a mast to which the upper end of *shrouds* are attached.
Tender: (1) A boat is said to be tender if it *heels* readily. 2) A boat's dinghy.
Tide: The rise and fall of sea levels due principally to the gravitational influence of the moon.
Tiller: A lever (usually of wood) attached to the top of the rudder, for the purpose of steering the boat.
Topsides: The exterior area of the hull between the *waterline* and the deck. Not the deck and cabin structure as is often believed.
Triatic stay: Part of the *standing rigging*. A wire leading from the top of one mast to the top of another, providing fore-and-aft support for the masts where there is more than one.
Trim: (1) To adjust the sails. 2) To adjust the weight distribution within the boat to alter its fore-and-aft angle of flotation.
Trimaran: A *multihull* boat with three hulls.

True wind: The actual direction of the wind as might be observed from a stationary position.

Turnbuckle: See **Rigging screw**.

Under way: A boat is said to be under way when it not moored in any way, at anchor, or aground.

Variation: The difference between true north and magnetic north.

Veer: (1) A clockwise change in wind direction.
(2) To let out anchor chain (or rope) in a controlled manner.

Wake: The turbulence *astern* as a boat passes through the water.

Waterline: The level on the hull at which the surface of the water would lie in still conditions.

Weather helm: The tendency of a boat to head up to *windward*. Opposite of *lee helm*.

Wetted surface area: The area of the hull in contact with the water.

Whisker pole: A light pole used to hold out the *clew* of a *headsail*.

Winch: A drum-like device, turned by a handle, for winding in ropes.

Windage: The area of a boat above the *waterline* not contributing to its forward drive — e.g. everything except the sails.

Windlass: A *winch* used to haul up the anchor chain.

Windward: Towards the direction of the wind. The windward side of a boat is that exposed to the wind. Opposite of *leeward*.

Wing-and-wing: See Goosewing.

Yawl: A two-masted boat with the mizzen stepped right aft — correctly, aft of the rudder post or stock.

UNITED KINGDOM - USEFUL ADDRESSES

American Bureau of Shipping (Europe) Ltd.
ABS House, No. 1 Frying Pan Alley, London. E1 7HR
Tel: (071) 247 3255,
Fax: (071) 377 2453

Andrew Simpson & Associates
Davis's Boatyard, Cobb's Quay, Hamworthy, Poole, Dorset. BH15 4EJ
Tel: (0202) 670754,
Mobile: (0836) 570628
Fax: (0202) 671705

Cruising Association
Ivory House,St Katherine's Dock, London. E1 9AT .Tel: (071) 481 0881

H M Coastguard
Sunley House,90-93 High Holborn, London. WC1V 6LP.
Tel: (071) 405 6911

Island Cruising Club
The Island, Salcombe, Devon. TQ8 8DR
Tel: (054 884) 3481
Fax: (054 884) 3929

International Yacht Racing Union
60 Knightsbridge, Westminster, London. SW1X 7JX

Little Ship Club
Bell Wharf Lane, Upper Thames Street, London. EC4R 3TB
Tel: (071) 236 7729

Lloyds Register
71 Fenchurch Street, London. EC3M 4BS.Tel: (071) 709 9166

Marinecall
Dewhurst House,London. EC1A 9DL
Tel: (071) 236 3500

Multihull Offshore Cruising & Racing Association
28 Keynshambury Road, Cheltenham, Gloucestershire, GL52 6HB
Tel: (0242) 511982

NFSS - National Federation of Sea Schools
Staddlestones, Fletchwood Lane, Totton, Southampton. SO4 2DZ
Tel: (0703) 869956

Ocean Cruising Club
6 Creek End, Emsworth, Hampshire. PO10 7EX. Tel: (0243) 378539

Ocean Youth Club
The Bus Station, South Street, Gosport, Hampshire. PO12 1EP

Registrar of British Shipping
H M Customs & Excise, Portcullis House, (0860) 433163
21 Cowbridge Road East, Cardiff. CF1 9SS.
Tel: (0222) 238531, Ext 4143
Note: Addresses of all other Registry Ports may be obtained from Cardiff.

RNLI - Royal National Lifeboat Institution
Headquarters, West Quay Road, Poole, Dorset. BH15 1HZ
Tel: (0202) 671133

RORC - Royal Ocean Racing Club
20 St James Place, London. SW1A 1MN
Tel: (071) 493 2248

RYA - Royal Yachting Association
RYA House, Romsey Road, Eastleigh, Hampshire. SO5 4YA.
Tel: (0703) 629962

Sail Training Association
5 Mumby Road, Gosport, Hampshire. PO12 1AA.
Tel: (0705) 586367

SSR - Small Ships Register
c/o Royal Yachting Association, RYA House,Romsey Road,Eastleigh, Hampshire. SO5 4YA.
Tel: (0703) 644061

Yacht Brokers, Designers & Surveyors Association
Wheel House, Petersfield Road, Whitehill, Bordon, Hampshire.
Tel: (0420) 473862,
Fax: (0420) 488328

Yacht Charter Association
60 Silverdale, New Milton,
Hampshire. BH25 7DE
Tel: (0425) 619004

UNITED STATES - USEFUL ADDRESSES

American Boat & Yacht Council, Inc.
PO Box 806, 190 Ketcham Avenue,
Amityville, New York. 11701

American Bureau of Shipping
45 Eisenhower Drive, Paramus,
New Jersey. 07653-0910
Tel: (201) 368 9100,
Fax: (201) 368-0255

Boat Owners Association of the United States (BOAT/US)
880 S Pickett Street, Alexandria,
Virginia. 22304

Cruising Club of America
c/o Pratt, Read & Co.,
Ivoryton, Connecticut. 06442

National Safe Boating Council, Secretary,
U S Coast Guard HQ G-BBS-4,
2100 2nd Street SW,
Washington DC. 20593

Slocum Society
P.O. Box 76, Port Townsend,
WA 98369

U S Coastguard
Coastguard Headquarters,
400 7th Street, NW
Washington DC. 20591
Tel: (202) 2672229

U S Coastguard
Marine Inspection Office, New York,
Battery Park Building,
New York, NY 10004.
Tel: (212) 6687000/1
Fax: (202) 668 3362

U S Coastguard Auxiliary
c/o Commandant (G-BAU),
Washington, DC. 20593-0001

United States Power Squadrons
P O Box 30423, Raleigh,
North Carolina. 27622

U S Yacht Racing Union
1133 Avenue of the Americas,
New York, NY 10036

Index